Contents

Turbulence

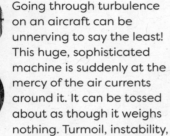

Going through turbulence on an aircraft can be unnerving to say the least! This huge, sophisticated machine is suddenly at the mercy of the air currents around it. It can be tossed about as though it weighs nothing. Turmoil, instability, upheaval, disorder, chaos – all of these capture something of the meaning of turbulence.

In this issue both John Grayston and Elaine Duncan use the word 'turbulent' in their separate *Way In* articles on Jeremiah, describing the period of Jewish history in which he wrote. But it's a word which could apply equally to our other series of readings. Roger Combes continues Alison Allen's notes on Matthew, leading us through the most turbulent few days in human history, during which Jesus suffered, died and rose again.

Michele Smart reminds us that Revelation was written for a small group of young churches which were 'on a collision course with the might of Rome' – turbulence ahead for them for sure! But Penny Boshoff continues the story as Jesus gives John (and us!) a revelation of the spiritual realities behind our turbulent world and what lies ahead.

Perhaps turbulence is the experience of most churches from time to time. It was certainly the case in Corinth as David Bracewell and Phil Winn show us from 2 Corinthians. But it also resulted in some of Paul's most moving and pastoral writing. In our lives as Christians, turbulence can be surprisingly productive!

Finally, James Davies gives a preview of the next *Daily Bread* with yet more turbulence, this time in the life of King David from 2 Samuel. Fasten your seat belts!

'Tricia and Emlyn Williams
Editors

Daily Bread toolbox

Tricia & Emlyn Williams worked with Scripture Union for many years. Emlyn led Schools ministry, then worked with SU International. Tricia was also part of the schools team and later worked for SU Publishing, developing, writing and editing Bible resources. Having recently completed research in the area of faith and dementia, he continues with writing and editing faith resources. Retired from his role as discipleship pastor in a local church, Emlyn now continues his writing and talking-with-people ministries.

WAY IN

This page introduces both the notes and the writer. It sets the scene and tells you what you need to know to get into each series.

A DAY'S NOTE

The notes for each day include five key elements: *Prepare*, *Read* (the Bible passage for the day), *Explore*, *Respond* and *Bible in a year*. These are intended to provide a helpful way of meeting God in his Word.

PREPARE

Prepare yourself to meet with God and pray that the Holy Spirit will help you to understand and respond to what you read.

READ

Read the Bible passage, taking time to absorb and simply enjoy it. A verse or two from the Bible text is usually included on each page, but it's important to read the whole passage.

EXPLORE

Explore the meaning of the passage, listening for what God may be saying to you. Before you read the comment, ask yourself: what is the main point of this passage? What is God showing me about himself or about my life? Is there a promise or a command, a warning or example to take special notice of?

RESPOND

Respond to what God has shown you in the passage in worship and pray for yourself and others. Decide how to share your discoveries with others.

BIBLE IN A YEAR

If your aim is to know God and his Word more deeply, why not follow this plan and read the whole Bible in one year?

Hope and hot chocolate

Joel Barwick is a youth worker with St Thomas's church in Newcastle city centre. After meeting SU Mission Enabler Geoff Brown and hearing about the Revealing Jesus mission framework, Joel became a Faith Guide. We asked him about how it has changed his outlook and experiences of mission.

How and why did you become a Faith Guide?

'Soon after I arrived in Newcastle in 2019, I linked up with SU Local Mission Partner MINE. We got some funding from SU's Good News Fund to trial some detached youth work in deprived areas. It's the one kind of youth work that's been permitted during pandemic lockdowns, so we've been able to continue doing it. And through it, I met Geoff from SU. He told me about the Revealing Jesus mission framework and invited me to become a Faith Guide – I jumped at the opportunity!

'I'm really fortunate to get great support from my church, but Scripture Union are the experts in doing mission with young people and it's so good to be able to tap into that expertise. The mission framework and the Connect, Explore, Respond and Grow phases bring some welcome structure to work with. Even as you're planning how to connect with young people, it gets you thinking ... how that might play out into the 'Grow' stage. It's helped me to think longer-term and has given me more focus.

'You also get access to all SU's resources to use with young people at different stages of the journey. You're assigned an SU Mission Enabler (Geoff, in my case) and it's so good to have this wisdom and support. It's been great to work with other Faith Guides in the local area as well, to chat and share ideas.'

What's youth work looked like for you since you became a Faith Guide?

'The pandemic's limited what we can do, so we've been doing detached youth work, going down to a park in Walker (a deprived area of Newcastle) at 6pm each Friday for an hour. There are usually between five and 30 young people, aged as young as 8. Even in torrential rain and freezing temperatures there are still young people out on the streets. We suspect they don't have the safest of spaces at home and feel more comfortable on the streets, even in bad weather.

'It's an opportunity to be a light in their lives. We take down hot chocolate and snacks and, now they know us, they run up all excited. We might do a bit of socially distanced sport and chat, and sometimes we use SU Rooted Cards – they're great for starting conversations.

'The kids are opening up to us now, and some of their situations are heart-breaking. One Friday night it was really tipping down and Spencer, this little lad of 10, turns up on his scooter, having travelled from his home about 2 miles away. We gave him a packet of crisps, but he wouldn't eat them. When I asked him why not, he said, "Because I want to give them to my mum, because we've run out of food." His mum's single, and she's got five kids under 14. Their rent had tripled that week and she had nothing left to buy food. We took them food that night and arranged for a food bank to keep them supplied.

'Now Spencer comes to see us every Friday in the park. We've also started a homework club with him because he struggles with school. So although it's a heart-breaking situation, we just feel as though God put him in our path.

'Another lad, Jimmy, told me, "I just want to live at home with my mum and two sisters. I used to live with my dad, but he was too noisy." When I asked what he meant, Jimmy said, "He got drunk all the time and the other week he tried to burn the house down. So the police had to take him away." Jimmy is just 8 years old. I didn't even know what drunk was when I was 8 years old. But this is the harsh reality that these young people face. And we passionately want them to be able to experience God's love.'

SU article

Do you have any sense of how the next mission framework stages – Explore, Respond and Grow – might develop?

'We're still at the Connect stage through the detached youth work, but I can see the homework club graduating towards the Explore stage. I think other needs will emerge as we get to know the kids more. Whatever comes next has to be shaped by them. So we're really open to what it might be.

'But we're already exploring doing some new missional work involving a combination of face-to-face work in schools and online ministry. I'm trying to marry the two together and learn from what we've had to do during the pandemic. Youth mission involves going to where young people hang out, and the place where there are most young people is online. They're playing video games; they're on TikTok; they're on Instagram; they're on Snapchat. Even children as young as 8 have their own phones. So there's a harvest field online and we need to be speaking the gospel there and sharing it effectively. Those young people are going to be learning about the world and life through worldly things unless we go on to those digital platforms and teach them differently.

'You still need the face-to-face work though. You can do the Connect stage with young people online, but I really feel you need a personal relationship for the Explore and Respond stages of a faith journey. And you need that too for the Grow stage – you need someone to

disciple you, to walk alongside you and help you to mature as a Christian.'

Would you recommend being a Faith Guide?

'Absolutely. I think when it comes to youth work, some churches aren't sure what they can offer or where to start. It can be a really big block for them.

'Having the Revealing Jesus mission framework and someone to lead you through putting it into practice is hugely beneficial. I can pick up the phone to Geoff, sound him out on my ideas and he'll help me improve on them. Not only that: he'll come and lend a hand too. At the moment he's out every Friday night, chatting to the young people right alongside me – I'm blown away by how servant-hearted SU people are.'

Find out more about the Revealing Jesus mission framework and being a Faith Guide! We're looking for volunteers, commissioned by their local church and supported by Scripture Union, to act as Faith Guides for children and young people without church backgrounds, walking alongside them as they journey to faith. Could that be you, or someone you know? Find out more and apply at su.org.uk/becomeafaithguide

A shorter version of this story first appeared in Connecting You, *SU's free quarterly supporter and prayer magazine. Subscribe for free, to learn more of how God is moving in the hearts and lives of children and young people today: su.org.uk/connectingyou*

Scripture Union

IT'S YOUR MOVE

YOUR SECONDARY SCHOOL SURVIVAL GUIDE

- Over 2 million children helped to settle into a new school through this series.
- A great way to support children in your local schools.
- Includes a survival guide, survival journal and survival stories to help children adapt to a new school.
- Additional content available online.

Scripture Union

IT'S YOUR MOVE

YOUR SECONDARY SCHOOL SURVIVAL GUIDE

ORDER FROM **YOUR LOCAL CHRISTIAN BOOKSHOP**
ORDER FROM **SCRIPTURE UNION: 01908 856006**
ORDER ONLINE **WWW.SCRIPTUREUNION.ORG.UK**

Waiting for his coming

About the writer
Alison Allen

After 14 years involved in mission in and from Romania, Alison returned to the UK in 2014 and now lives in Suffolk with her husband, two young children and three cats. Alison is currently working in the local Public Health department, whilst researching millennials in international mission for a PhD.

Over the next week, we will be looking at two chapters from Matthew's Gospel known as the 'Olivet Discourse', in which Jesus prophesies about the destruction of Jerusalem and the end of this age. We will be shocked by great suffering and challenged to be on the alert. These chapters have been interpreted in numerous ways, and many have tried to answer the disciples' question in Matthew 24:3: 'When will this happen, and what will be the sign?'

As the events of the Covid-19 pandemic unfolded around the world, a lot of apocalyptic language was used in an attempt to explain what was going on. Some suggested that the end was near, others that it was judgement for sin. For many of us, we could suddenly relate to the people in Noah's days, eating and drinking and getting married (24:38) until disaster struck. With these events fresh in our memories, this is a good time to look at what Jesus actually said. Perhaps living through a global pandemic has given us a new perspective on the instability of this life and on the hope that we have as Christians for a future that is certain.

Whether we live through pandemics, natural disasters, war or personal tragedy, our question should not be the extent to which current events relate to prophecies in Matthew, Daniel or Revelation, but simply whether we are ready today if Jesus either returns or calls us home. When he comes, will he find us doing what he has asked us to do (24:46)?

Great things for God

PREPARE
Count your blessings! Thank God for the ways in which he has blessed you.

READ
Matthew 25:14–30

EXPLORE

This is a parable we may hear often. It's a simple story about making good use of what you have been given. What we perhaps don't hear so often is the context: it is very much part of this section on Jesus' second coming. The word 'again' in verse 14 clearly links this story to what comes before (a different version might use 'for' or something similar). Jesus is reiterating here the two main points from our previous passages: we cannot know when he will return, and we should live as if it might be today.

I think this perspective slightly alters our understanding. It's not that we are to use *our* resources and *our* abilities for God; rather, all that we have remains in *his* ownership and has simply been entrusted to our care for a time. One day we will be asked to give him an account of what we have done (v 19) with his possessions.

In his call to world missions in 1792, William Carey said we should expect great things from God and attempt great things for God. We're not expected to do things for God without first receiving from him. As God entrusts things into our hands, we are to set to work with them (v 27). If we are faithful in using what God gives us, we will be given increasing responsibility (v 29).

> 'Again, it will be like a man going on a journey, who called his servants and entrusted his wealth to them.'
>
> **Matthew 25:14**

RESPOND
What has God entrusted you with? How are you investing those things?

Spot the difference

PREPARE
Pray for the leaders of your local church.

- -

READ
Matthew 25:31–46

EXPLORE

I sometimes take my children to visit a local farm which specialises in rare breeds. In some cases, it's remarkably difficult to tell the sheep and goats apart. These are the kind of sheep and goats Jesus' contemporaries would have been familiar with. A shepherd would have had one mixed flock, and all the animals were similar in size and colour, all with little horns. They could not easily be told apart just by looking. Separating them required the skill and knowledge of the shepherd (vs 32,33). Jesus' point seems to be that it's not about appearances, but rather about the actions of the individuals concerned. Only the King himself – the Good Shepherd now on his throne – sees the hearts of all people.

This passage has been interpreted in different ways. Some understand 'the least of these [my] brothers and sisters' (v 40) as the poor in general, others as needy Jews, and still others as Christians in need. I guess it doesn't really matter. If we are seeking to follow the commands and example of Jesus throughout the Gospels – not just trying to meet the minimum requirements to be placed on his right at the judgement – then we will care for the poor and needy regardless of religion. This really matters to Jesus. We can't just look like his sheep without doing the things his sheep should do.

'…"Truly I tell you, whatever you did for one of the least of these brothers and sisters of mine, you did for me."'
Matthew 25:40

RESPOND
Ask the Lord to show you what part you can play in caring for the hungry, the sick, prisoners and others in need.

- -

Bible in a year: Joshua 4,5; Romans 10

Faithful God

PREPARE
There are a lot of songs about God's faithfulness – sing or say the words of your favourite!

READ
Psalm 40

EXPLORE
David wrote this psalm as he faced many troubles, apparently caused by his own sin (v 12). We don't know the exact context, but he is clearly waiting and hoping for deliverance (vs 11,13).

If you were to stop reading at verse 10, you'd think David's troubles were all in the past. He describes how God hears him (v 1) and delivers him (v 2). He talks about singing God's praises (v 3), doing his will (v 8) and telling others about him (vs 9,10). It doesn't sound like the song of someone whose life is under threat (v 14) and whose heart is failing because he is overwhelmed by sin and evil (v 12). But it is.

I don't think David is trying to twist God's arm, trying to force the Lord to rescue him because of the past record of either of them. No, David is rehearsing to himself God's goodness and faithfulness. At this time, again in desperate need,

he is reminding himself of how God has delivered him previously. When life is hard, let's look back on the ways God has intervened in our lives in the past, instead of focusing on our troubles and feeling as if God has abandoned us. He is the same yesterday, today and for ever (Hebrews 13:8). We stand on a rock (v 2b).

> Do not withhold your mercy from me, LORD; may your love and faithfulness always protect me.

Psalm 40:11

RESPOND
Take time to remember some specific instances of God's goodness to you in the past. Praise him!

Bible in a year: Joshua 6,7; Romans 11

The pioneer of our faith

About the writer
Roger Combes

Roger has ministered in London, Cambridge and East and West Sussex. He and his wife live in Crawley, near Gatwick airport and glorious countryside. Being retired means he can now watch more sport of all kinds. He has supported Bournemouth football club for 60 years.

I was a bit surprised when the vicar said, 'We do not serve an ever-living saviour.' But, of course, he was right. We serve a saviour who suffered, died and was buried; then he was raised from the dead and, praise God, is alive for evermore. In the next fortnight, we read the last three chapters of Matthew's Gospel, which give us a full account, in 161 verses, of the suffering, death and resurrection of Jesus of Nazareth.

We shall accompany him, day by day, as he pioneers his solitary way to the cross and through death for us. We shall watch as nearly everyone withdraws their support from him – disciples, the crowd, the religious authorities, the Roman governor and, in the end, even his heavenly Father (Matthew 27:46). It is infinitely shocking. The Lord Jesus is intensely human, and sensitive both to the malice and to the needs of the different people around him. Consistently he shows love, understanding, self-control and faithfulness to God and neighbour. It is compelling to read and very humbling. We are drawn not just to admire him but to worship him.

As we turn to this timeless story, we might echo the words of Godfrey Birtill's song: 'I will set my face to seek the Lord … I will listen for his voice: my Wonderful Counsellor, my Teacher … my Inspirer … my Jesus, my Saviour, my wonderful God.'

Hostility and love

PREPARE

In our passage today we read about a woman who 'came to Jesus' (v 7). Let's bring ourselves to him anew, as we read and pray.

READ

Matthew 26:1–16

EXPLORE

Jesus is about to face his biggest test, and everything depends on what happens in the coming days. Matthew, our commentator and expert summariser, introduces us (vs 1–5) to the main players. There's Jesus, of course, who will die centre-stage. And the chief priests, a nasty lot. The crowd, vocal but unreliable. And key disciples, women and men, particularly Judas (vs 14–16). They will be unforgettable participants in Jesus' approaching ordeal.

As for the background, Jesus will have to cope with a conspiracy to murder on the one hand (vs 4,14–16) and devoted love on the other (vs 6–12). Most of us are not at our best when being criticised or plotted against. But Jesus was. Despite the hostility, he calmly rebuffed the criticism from his disciples about the values, and the value, of the woman anointing him. Others of us are sometimes awkward or big-headed when we are shown appreciation. Not so Jesus. He remained unruffled, and affirmed the woman who had lavished her precious perfume on him.

As for the woman, she took her opportunity to show her love to her Lord when she could. If she had put it off for a week, she would have been too late.

'As you know, the Passover is two days away – and the Son of Man will be handed over to be crucified.'

Matthew 26:2

RESPOND

If you don't have an alabaster jar of precious perfume handy, what could you bring to the Lord to show how much you appreciate him?

Matthew 26:17–25

Passover preparations

PREPARE
Listening to the Lord can make us more resilient in the future. Be attentive to what he says today.

READ
Matthew 26:17–25

EXPLORE
Good meals require good preparation. Jesus planned ahead for this private meal with the 12 disciples. He had 'booked' the room. His mention of 'my appointed time' (v 18) suggests that he was also conscious of working to his Father's plan. Preparing this Passover meal would take up most of what we often call Maundy Thursday.

Then Jesus set about preparing his disciples. They were in for some big shocks in the next 72 hours. He had already broken the news to them that he would soon be executed (eg verse 2), and now he revealed something else that would shock them: 'One of you will betray me' (v 21). They were stunned. They had no suspicions concerning Judas. He was there reclining in the room with them, with 30 silver coins in his pocket (vs 14,15), and protesting, like the others, 'Not me, surely?'

We cannot be certain why Judas turned against Jesus. Perhaps Judas himself did not fully know. Jesus here teaches his disciples two things about God and evil. First, God's good purpose *will* be carried out, 'as it is written' (v 24a). Secondly, human beings can act wickedly (v 24b). Both are true, even if we can't reconcile them. Jesus held on to both at the same time.

> 'The Son of Man will go just as it is written about him. But woe to that man who betrays the Son of Man!'
>
> **Matthew 26:24**

RESPOND
Thank the Lord for those times when you realise he was graciously preparing you for things in your life still to come.

Bible in a year: Joshua 10,11; Psalm 38

Bread, wine and bravado

PREPARE

The poem 'Love Bade Me Welcome' (George Herbert, 1593–1633) beautifully illustrates Christ's desire that we should meet with him. May its ending illustrate our response: 'So I did sit and eat.'

READ

Matthew 26:26–35

EXPLORE

How do you feel when people ignore what you say? It happened to Jesus during his last meal. Jesus lovingly gave Judas a solemn warning that it was better not to be born than to betray the Son of Man (v 24). Judas took no notice. Jesus predicted that the disciples would all desert him that night (v 31). They contradicted him. Jesus said that Peter would disown him (vs 33–35). 'Never,' said Peter. But Jesus was right. They all failed him, as disciples tend to do without the help of the Holy Spirit (Acts 2). Even when Jesus spoke encouragingly of his resurrection (v 32) and the heavenly banquet (v 29), they seemed to ignore these words too.

By contrast, the annual Passover meal spoke of God's faithfulness. It reminded the people of the Lord's covenant: that he was their God, and they were his people. Jesus now tells his disciples that God's covenant specifically includes 'the forgiveness of sins' – how wonderful to hear those words from the lips of Jesus (v 28)! Most covenants were made with an animal sacrifice. So, imagine the shock when Jesus spoke of '*my* blood' of the covenant. Jesus himself was its sacrificial lamb. The bread and wine of the Lord's Supper make real to us his body broken and his blood shed for us. Such is his faithfulness to us.

'This is my blood of the covenant, which is poured out for many for the forgiveness of sins.'

Matthew 26:28

RESPOND

How receptive are you towards Christ? How faithful are you in receiving his word and sacrament?

Bible in a year: Joshua 12–15; Romans 13

Jesus alone

PREPARE
Perhaps we should take off our shoes. Today's passage is holy ground.

READ
Matthew 26:36–46

EXPLORE

'Don't go. Stay with me.' It's the sort of plea someone might breathe if they are feeling weak or vulnerable. It's a very human reaction. In Gethsemane, Jesus was deeply saddened. He said to Peter, James and John: 'My soul is overwhelmed with sorrow to the point of death. Stay here and keep watch with me' (v 38). Remarkably, the Son of God wanted the human companionship of these three fishermen. When, later, he found them asleep, it can only have added to his sense of wretchedness. We might note in passing that being holy and in the centre of God's will – as the Lord Jesus undoubtedly was – may include times of being deeply troubled.

We have all prayed the prayer Jesus prayed – in the Lord's Prayer: 'Your will be done.' Jesus prayed it here at least three times (vs 39,42,44), because he was determined to carry out his Father's wish. But he also wanted, and he pleaded in prayer, to be spared 'this cup', the awful trial of suffering facing him. He was appalled by it, as any sensitive soul would be. His prayer was heard. But the answer was 'No'.

Jesus was human like us. Like us, he needed human companionship. Like us, he prayed to avoid suffering. Like us, he wanted to do as his Father wished.

'My Father, if it is possible, may this cup be taken from me. Yet not as I will, but as you will.'
Matthew 26:39

RESPOND
Resolve that your trust in your heavenly Father will be constant, even if, like Jesus, you do not receive what you earnestly pray for.

Bible in a year: Joshua 16–19; Romans 14

'It must happen this way'

PREPARE
Commit your way to the Lord (Psalm 37:5): always a good first step in anything.

- -

READ
Matthew 26:47–56

EXPLORE
It must have been scary. At least one disciple had a sword. An armed crowd was approaching in the dark. The familiar figure of Judas emerged and identified Jesus as the one to arrest. Did it surprise Judas that Jesus called him 'friend' (v 50)?

Why didn't Jesus resist arrest? He could have walked through the crowd unharmed, as he had before in Nazareth (Luke 4:28–30). He could have tried physical force (v 52) or avoided the garden that night. He could have called on thousands of angels to rescue him (v 53). That would have worked.

It is part of Matthew's good news that God's eternal plan for the world was now happening. Twice already in this chapter he has pointed out that the events were taking place 'as it is written' (vs 24,31). Jesus says the same here. He was going the way the Scriptures had set out for him (vs 54,56). If he were to be rescued, how would the Scriptures be fulfilled (v 54)? Jesus believed his Old Testament Scriptures, and so may we. He deliberately chose to follow them and give himself up for others. We may ask ourselves: if the Son of God submitted himself to obeying the Scriptures, how much more should we?

'But how then would the Scriptures be fulfilled that say it must happen in this way?'
Matthew 26:54

RESPOND
What is your overriding aim in life? Make Christ's ambition your own: 'I have come to do your will, my God' (Hebrews 10:7).

Bible in a year: Joshua 20–22; Psalm 39

Are *you* the Messiah?

PREPARE

'But the Lord stood at my side and gave me strength' (2 Timothy 4:17). Pray for this to be true in any trial you are facing.

READ

Matthew 26:57–68

EXPLORE

It was not easy for Caiaphas, the high priest, to manipulate things to get Jesus killed. The top Jewish Council, the Sanhedrin, of which he was president, could not itself exact the death penalty. Caiaphas had to find compelling charges against Jesus that would carry the death penalty both from the Roman governor under Roman law (eg sedition), and also from the Sanhedrin under Jewish law (eg blasphemy). But the testimony from witnesses was unconvincing, and the accused was exercising his right to silence. The only hope for Caiaphas was to get Jesus to incriminate himself.

Jesus obliged (vs 63b,64). He declared under oath to the leaders of God's people that he was far more exalted than their ideas of 'Messiah' and 'Son of God'. He was (and is) the divine 'son of man' of Daniel 7:9–14, coming on the clouds of heaven to the throne of God to be served by all the world and to reign with glory, authority and an everlasting dominion that will not pass away.

This was a far better 'confession' than Caiaphas could have imagined! He got his 'blasphemy' verdict (vs 65,66). Jesus then suffered further indignities (vs 67,68). The one we worship is no stranger to humiliation, injustice and brutality.

'… you will see the Son of Man sitting at the right hand of the Mighty One and coming on the clouds of heaven.'

Matthew 26:64

RESPOND

'Accept our praises, Lord Jesus Christ, the faithful witness, who stood in our world enduring trumped-up charges, lies from witnesses and bias from the establishment. Amen.'

Bible in a year: Joshua 23,24; Romans 15

Blessed are the merciful

PREPARE
Pray to be filled with God's Spirit for the various demands of the coming week.

READ
Psalm 41

EXPLORE
Question: Whom does the Lord deliver, protect, preserve, bless, sustain and restore?

Answer: Those who 'have regard for the weak' (vs 1–3). 'Have regard' means more than making a casual donation. It means taking trouble and giving serious thought to what can be done for people in need. The Lord himself is a friend to the vulnerable. It is in his character, and he blesses the same trait in his people. 'Blessed are the merciful,' said Jesus (Matthew 5:7) 'for they will be shown mercy.'

The psalmist's life was blighted by two things: a debilitating illness and opponents who were taking advantage of it (vs 3–9). Sinner that he was, he looked to the Lord for mercy (vs 4,10) to help with both problems. If this was David the king speaking, it could be at a time of uprising in his kingdom. How he longed for the strength to be able to put things right! How frustrating that he couldn't! Verse 9 tells us that a former friend had turned against him very *un*mercifully. Jesus pondered this verse when Judas turned against him (John 13:18).

The psalmist knows he can count on the pleasure and the presence of the Lord (vs 11,12). He calls on him for his merciful support (v 10).

Blessed are those who have regard for the weak; the LORD delivers them in times of trouble.
Psalm 41:1

RESPOND
Thank you, Lord, that you bless those who bless the weak. Show me how I can help any who are sick or unfairly treated. Amen.

Bible in a year: Judges 1,2; Romans 16

Peter alone and in tears

PREPARE
Take heart that the Lord does not give up on us because we have failed him.

READ
Matthew 26:69–75

EXPLORE

Peter the fisherman found himself outside the high priest's house, a place oozing with influence and wealth. The sophisticated elite of Jerusalem had just decided to apply the death penalty to Jesus (v 66). Did Peter find his confidence draining away?

This was the most shameful incident of his life. Hours before, he had insisted that he would rather die than deny his Lord. But now, facing banter from strangers, he denied that he had been Jesus' friend and colleague for three wonderful years. He denied even that he knew Jesus. He emphatically refused to identify with Jesus.

Was Peter simply emotionally exhausted after a busy evening: the Last Supper, Judas' betrayal, failing Jesus in Gethsemane, drawing his sword and nearly killing someone (John 18:10), and seeing Jesus roughed up by court bullies (vs 67,68)? Can you imagine yourself being cowed into denying Christ by the people around you? Or by unfamiliar surroundings? Or by the dazzle of power? Or by a sense of inferiority? Or...? The fact is there was no good reason for Peter not to identify bravely with Jesus of Nazareth.

Peter's sobbing marked real repentance (v 75). He made no secret of his sin. The church came to know all about it. It's in all four Gospels. His Lord knew it too, and forgave. (See Mark 16:7; John 21:15–17.)

> Then Peter ... went outside and wept bitterly.
>
> **Matthew 26:75**

RESPOND
'Oh, that it might be said of me, "Surely your speech gives you away; you have been with Jesus of Galilee!"'*

*CSSM chorus by EHG Sargent (adapted).

Bible in a year: Judges 3,4; Mark 1

The cupboard was bare

PREPARE

'Before thy throne we sinners bend – grace, pardon, life to us extend.'* Lord, in your mercy, hear our prayer.

READ

Matthew 27:1–10

EXPLORE

Judas is in a bad way. He is racked with regret. He hates himself. He hates the sordid money he was paid. He has seen Jesus led away for sentencing, and blurts out before the chief priests, 'I have betrayed innocent blood' (vs 3,4a). And they reply, in effect, 'Not our problem' (v 4b). If your church minister spoke like that to someone who was broken inside because of something they had done, what would you think?

When Judas turned up at the Temple full of remorse and needing restoration, there was no one to help him. The Temple leaders had nothing to offer. Their cupboard was bare. They were as lost as Judas. Judas did not know how to get back to Jesus, the gracious friend of sinners. He never saw the cross.

The days of the Temple were coming to an end. God had commanded it to be the place of regular sacrifices for sin, but now there was a better sacrifice coming, to take away the sin of the world. It was not far away. Just outside the city wall. The place to find God was shifting. Now we do not go to the Temple, but to the cross; in fact, not to a place, but to a person; not to a system, but to a saviour.

Blessed is the one who does not walk in step with the wicked.

Psalm 1:1

RESPOND

Have you ever been in despair? What has that experience shown you about helping people when they are in trouble?

*'Father of Heaven, Whose Love Profound', E. Cooper (1770–1833)

Bible in a year: Judges 5,6; Psalms 40,41

'That innocent man'

PREPARE

As Good Friday draws near, let's concentrate our attention on Jesus, who 'For the joy that was set before him ... endured the cross, scorning its shame' (Hebrews 12:2).

READ

Matthew 27:11–26

EXPLORE

Jesus probably didn't get much sleep that night, and then it was a dawn start for the next day, the day of his death. After an early morning strategy meeting (Matthew 27:1,2), the chief priests ratified the death sentence of the night before (Luke 22:66), and Jesus was taken for a trial under Roman justice.

Have you ever faced unfair or unjust treatment? Or manipulation, or vested interest? Or public opinion attacking you? Or pressure to 'confess' falsely? Or a judge too weak to do the right thing? Or physical assault? The Lord Jesus endured all this.

Jesus' fate, legally speaking, was in the hands of one man, Pontius Pilate, the Roman governor. Pilate felt trapped. His duty, clearly, was to acquit the innocent and yet also to keep the peace. He knew that Jesus was innocent of the charges against him (vs 19,23), but also that he (Pilate) had been out-manoeuvred by the high priests (v 18) and a riot might start. The crowd had turned against Jesus of Nazareth. Shouts of 'Crucify! Crucify!' echoed in his ears. Pilate washed his hands, trying to evade blame. Jesus watched, and, after hearing his sentence, was taken away. The cross before him, no turning back.

> ... and the governor asked him, 'Are you the king of the Jews?' 'You have said so,' Jesus replied.
>
> **Matthew 27:11**

RESPOND

'O make me understand it, / help me to take it in; / what it meant to thee, the Holy One, / to take away my sin.'*

*'Give me a Sight O Saviour', Katherine Agnes May Kelly (1869–1942)

Bible in a year: Judges 7,8; Mark 2

Mocked and crucified

PREPARE

'Jesus, lifted up to die, draw me to yourself. Amen.'

READ

Matthew 27:27–44

EXPLORE

No one could resist poking fun at Jesus that day. Everyone was doing it. If you have ever been bullied (or in the past have bullied someone else), you may recognise the urge to belittle a victim who cannot defend themselves.

The first to mock Jesus was the highly respectable Sanhedrin Jewish Council the night before. They spat in his face, struck, slapped and taunted him (26:67,68). Then it was Pilate's men, Gentile soldiers from different nations. They gave 'king' Jesus a mock crown, a fancy-dress imperial robe and a rod of authority which they beat him with. They spat on him and paid fake homage to him (vs 28–30). The Roman governor himself was perhaps amused to label Jesus as the nation's king (v 37).

Casual passers-by joined in the mockery (vs 39,40), and even the chief priests and other leaders descended into gratuitous insult (vs 41–43). Did they realise that their clever 'put-downs' were predicted in Scripture, like so much else that day (eg Psalm 22:7,8,17,18)? Jesus' fellow criminals, crucified on either side of him, also piled abuse on him (v 44).

I once spent Lent and Easter abroad and on my own. I was perfectly happy, but alone. What spoke to me most that year was the cruelty in the taunts directed at the Lord Jesus, which he endured on his own.

> They spat on him, and took the staff and struck him on the head again and again.
>
> **Matthew 27:30**

RESPOND

When you see people bullying or making fun of someone, do you find yourself tending to side with the victim or the mockers? Remember Jesus.

Bible in a year: Judges 9,10; Mark 3

Friday 15 April
Matthew 27:45–56

The death of Jesus

PREPARE

Being present when someone dies is always humbling. Let us humble ourselves today as we watch the Lord Jesus breathe his last.

READ

Matthew 27:45–56

EXPLORE

How could God turn away from the Lord Jesus dying unjustly and helplessly on the cross? Surely the Father could not forsake his beloved Son in his hour of need? *But he did*. That is exactly what happened. That is the depth of horror that is Good Friday. Jesus shouts out the pain of his forsakenness in the words of Psalm 22, 'My God, my God, why have you forsaken me?' (v 46). A profound mystery indeed. How serious is sin if it required the death of the eternal Son to expunge it? How deep is divine love, in that it went to such lengths for people like us?

We will not be the first readers to be puzzled by some of the details of Matthew's narrative: darkness in the afternoon (v 45), earthquake (v 54), graves splitting open, bodies raised to life, appearing in the holy city (vs 51–53). These may seem more suited to the Day of the Lord and the supernatural beginnings of a new age. Perhaps

that is the point. Good Friday *is* that supernatural new beginning. God massively intervened.

At the moment Jesus died, the Temple's heavy barrier curtain was torn in two, from top to bottom (vs 50,51). This barrier into the Holy of Holies was comprehensively destroyed. The message was clear. Jesus' death had opened the kingdom of heaven so that all may go in.

About three in the afternoon Jesus cried out in a loud voice, '*Eli, Eli, lema sabachthani*?' (which means 'My God, my God, why have you forsaken me?').

Matthew 27:46

RESPOND

'Alleluia! What a saviour!'*

*'Man of Sorrows', P Bliss (1838–1876).

Bible in a year: Judges 11,12; Psalms 42,43

Sealed in a stone-cold tomb

PREPARE
Are you exhausted or jaded? Or sad? The Lord is at hand. Allow him time to heal and restore you.

READ
Matthew 27:57–66

EXPLORE
Where were the disciples when Jesus died? Some seem not to have been around, but others cared faithfully to the end, notably many of the women (vs 55,56). Have you noticed that when there is a crisis or challenge, some people come out of the woodwork and are worth their weight in gold? (And other people, whom you thought you could depend on, can't be seen for dust!)

At this point, Joseph of Arimathea stepped up (vs 57–60). He was a wealthy member of the Sanhedrin ruling council, but he was different; he was a secret disciple of Jesus (John 19:38). Now, he came out publicly as a disciple, when it was the hardest time to do so. Jesus was dead and disgraced. The 'establishment' had triumphed. Joseph had nothing to gain and everything to lose. But he was undaunted. He may have been the only disciple in Jerusalem with the influence to access Pilate and ask for Jesus' body.

Pilate agreed. Mary Magdalene and another Mary stayed and watched as Joseph buried their Lord (v 61). Love is stronger than death. Joseph's actions made him the first person in the world to serve the crucified Christ.

The tomb was placed under extra security (vs 62–66) to make sure Jesus stayed dead and buried.

'The Son of Man must suffer many things and be rejected … and he must be killed and on the third day be raised to life.'
Luke 9:22

RESPOND
Easter Eve is a day to learn to wait patiently. It would be a pity if we give up just before God sends the blessing.

Bible in a year: Judges 13,14; Mark 4

Sunday 17 April
Matthew 28:1–10

Come and see. He is risen

PREPARE
Jesus Christ is risen today! Alleluia! Praise God!

READ
Matthew 28:1–10

EXPLORE

This was no ordinary 'first day of the week'. It was the first day of a new era and a new creation. God was doing something unique. With all the trappings of the presence of God (earthquake, angel, 'appearance like lightning', clothes as white as snow) the scene is set. Mary Magdalene takes the lead, and we are drawn in. The women approach Jesus' tomb, and they are met by an angel, and later by the Lord himself (vs 2,3,5–7,9). How things have changed in two nights! The tomb is empty. Christ is risen, just as he said (eg Matthew 20:18,19). Hearts thumping, the women hurry away on their mission. The angel's words to them (vs 5–7) are for us as well (italics added).

'Don't be afraid.' God is at work. God's righteousness has defeated human wickedness. Christ has been raised from the dead, that we may be also. *'Come and see.'* Take a look. It bears investigation. It all points to the one who was dead and is now alive for evermore (Revelation 1:18). *'Go and tell'* the others to meet Jesus.

The angel said, 'Go.' The Lord said, 'Go.' The other disciples had to 'go' to Galilee. And they did 'go' (vs 7,10,16). The resurrection of Christ changed their world – and ours. We lift our hearts in praise for the Easter victory.

> 'He is not here; he has risen, just as he said. Come and see the place where he lay.'
>
> **Matthew 28:6**

RESPOND
Rejoice in a living Saviour. Pray for any you know who are bereaved or dying. Is there anywhere you should be 'going' as a disciple of the risen Christ?

Bible in a year: Judges 15,16; Mark 5

All... all... all... always

PREPARE
Worshipping the risen Lord includes listening to him and doing what he says.

READ
Matthew 28:11–20

EXPLORE
The next day everyone in Jerusalem knew that the tomb was empty. What had happened? Clearly *something* had happened. It would be interesting to know what the chief priests and elders thought had actually happened. They felt they had to invent a fake story about it. But the disciples, eventually, knew that Christ was risen from the dead. In the days that followed, they saw him alive on several occasions; he talked with them in both Jerusalem and Galilee; and he commissioned them to go and tell the world. Which they did.

Did you notice all the 'all's in the final verses? All authority (v 18), all nations (v 19), all I have commanded (v 20) and always (v 20). The Lord Jesus Christ is not to be limited or under-valued. There is nothing we face in heaven or earth that he does not have authority over. There is no nation or people group that is outside the scope of his good news.

He deserves the loving obedience of all our heart, all our soul, all our mind and all our strength. He doesn't just send you and me into the future; he comes with us all the time.

'Therefore go and make disciples of all nations, baptising them in the name of the Father and of the Son and of the Holy Spirit.'
Matthew 28:19

RESPOND
Think of a country whose name begins with the same letter as your own name. Then pray for it. (Between us, we should touch many nations!) Pray for new believers in that country, its pastors, its evangelists and those who suffer there.

Bible in a year: Judges 17,18; Mark 6

Jesus is Alive!

This Easter experience the amazing story of God's plan to save his people. Guardians of Ancora, developed by Scripture Union, is a free-to-download game that brings the stories of the Bible to life.

Experience the joy of knowing Jesus is alive and celebrate God's gift to all. Bring the story of the resurrection to life in the heart of a child this Easter. Download Guardians of Ancora for free and live the incredible adventures of Easter.

Download and **play**
Guardians of Ancora FOR FREE

Find out more at guardiansofancora.com

Scripture Union

God's love and God's pain

About the writer
John Grayston

Now retired after 37 years on the Scripture Union staff, John still writes, teaches and preaches. He is on the leadership team at Tile Kiln Church in Chelmsford. When he can he escapes to his allotment, or the mountains walking or skiing with his wife Jenny. He has two children and seven grandchildren.

Jeremiah lived and worked in one of the most turbulent periods in Jewish history. He was called to his prophetic role in 626 BC and his prophecies cover the reigns of the last five kings of Judah down to the Fall of Jerusalem in 587 BC. The first of these, Josiah, introduced reforms during which he found the Book of the Law in the Temple (2 Kings 22:1–13), but the rest ignored God. In the wider world Assyria was in decline, and Egypt and Babylon were the dominant powers with Judah trapped between them.

The northern kingdom of Israel fell in 722 BC, a result of turning away from God, but in the south Judah had failed to learn the lessons. They worshipped the local gods in the hope of guaranteed harvests. Oppression, injustice and a refusal to live by God's law were everywhere. The thrust of Jeremiah's message is that unless there is a return to God disaster will fall at the hands of an invader from the north.

Jeremiah's message was not a popular one. Our world is very different, but we still assert our independence and reject God. God, as he did through Jeremiah, still calls in grace for people to come back. And in Jesus we see that grace more clearly. No one is beyond God's love if only they will receive it. Our calling is to warn of the danger of ignoring God, to share the good news of his love and to call people to turn to God.

Tough call

PREPARE
Have you ever been asked to do something that you did not feel qualified for, or that you did not want to do? How did it feel?

READ
Jeremiah 1:1–19

EXPLORE

God has a job for Jeremiah. Great, we might think. But that wasn't Jeremiah's reaction. What God goes on to say doesn't sound too reassuring. Jeremiah has a hard message to bring: there will be uprooting and tearing down before any restoration can take place (v 10). The words will be Jeremiah's, reflecting his personality, experience and situation, but more importantly they will be words given to him by God.

God gives Jeremiah two pictures. An almond tree – the point being that God is watching (the Hebrew word for watching sounds like the Hebrew word for almond). God is in control and speaks into the situation. The boiling pot speaks of an enemy coming from the north – geography meant that Israel's enemies often did. The hard thing to take is that this is God's doing (v 15), a frequent theme in Jeremiah.

We are called to live and witness as God's people in a world which has turned its back on God. Our situation and our challenges are similar but not identical. People did not and do not listen. Like Jeremiah, we may face opposition and apathy, but we can be sure that God will do what he sets out to do.

> The Lord said to me, 'You have seen correctly, for I am watching to see that my word is fulfilled.'
> **Jeremiah 1:12**

RESPOND
What challenges are you facing as you live in a hostile world? Remember that God is watching and commit them to him.

Bible in a year: Judges 19,20; Psalm 44

Jilted God

PREPARE

I have titled this note 'Jilted God'. How do you react? Pray that you may gain an insight into God's heart.

READ

Jeremiah 2:1–19

EXPLORE

This is painful reading. God reminds Judah of her history. There were good times, but they are gone. The marriage has turned sour (v 2). Judah is no longer devoted to God (v 3). She has turned to worthless idols (vs 5,8). The climax is in verse 13. They have turned from the source of life and have tried to live in their own strength which proves totally inadequate. No other nation would dream of giving up on its gods, worthless though they are (v 11), but Judah has deserted the living God who brought them out of slavery in Egypt into a rich and fertile land.

This is humanity's sad story from Eden onwards: turning from God and believing that we can run our lives, we lose contact with the only source of life. Here we see the pain this causes God and we shall meet it again. How do we feel about the way that our world responds to God?

Judgement is never something that God wants; it is something that we bring on ourselves (v 19). It causes God pain. However much we shrink from it, it is a reality that we cannot ignore.

'My people have committed two sins: They have forsaken me, the spring of living water, and have dug their own cisterns, broken cisterns that cannot hold water.'

Jeremiah 2:13

RESPOND

Take a few moments to reflect on the pain that God feels when people turn their backs on him. As you begin to sense something of his grief, pray for your community.

Bible in a year: Judges 21; Mark 7

Faithless or faithful?

PREPARE
Acknowledge any sin or failure. Confess it and receive God's forgiveness.

READ
Jeremiah 3:6–25

EXPLORE
Like a repeated drumbeat, the word 'faithless' echoes through these verses – I counted six, and 'unfaithful' comes three times. This is the charge against Judah. Despite all that God has done for them, even though they have seen what happened to their northern neighbour Israel (vs 6–10), they have continued to worship other gods and to ignore God. There have been attempts at return, but they were superficial and lacked reality. Josiah had initiated a series of reforms (2 Kings 22:1 – 23:30), but they were not getting to the heart of the matter and most people were unchanged.

It might seem that there was no way back, but despite the continued faithlessness the door is still (just about) open. Three times God calls this faithless people to repent (vs 12,14,22). He takes the initiative in restoring the broken relationship. He offers the cure for their repeated rebellion (v 22). This is still true. There may come a time when God reluctantly and sadly closes the door – that time came for Judah – but for the moment it is open for any who will turn to God.

What God looks for is faithful living, a recognition of failure (v 13) and a return to God. Only then is there hope of salvation. For us as Christians this salvation comes through Jesus (Acts 4:12).

> 'Return, faithless people; I will cure you of backsliding.'
> **Jeremiah 3:22**

RESPOND
Turn verse 22 into a prayer for any you know who have turned away from God.

Bible in a year: Ruth 1,2; Mark 8

Uncomfortable God

PREPARE

We are about to read some hard verses. Ask God to help you face them honestly and meet with you as you read.

READ

Jeremiah 4:5–26

EXPLORE

Some years ago I was in a meeting where the leader invited us to call out qualities of God while he wrote them up. He then pointed out that we had all the comfortable qualities but words like 'anger' and 'judging' were missing. We can have a limited view of God. There are aspects of God that we would rather avoid. The picture in these verses of an angry God who judges his people is one of those. Different images of the invading army pile up: lion (v 7), scorching wind (vs 11,12), clouds, whirlwind, eagles (v 13). Terrible destruction is coming (vs 5,6). It is as though creation itself is being undone (vs 23–26; compare v 23 with Genesis 1:2 which uses the same Hebrew phrase). The ultimate horror is that all this is God's doing (v 8).

It may help us to remember that God is only angry because he cares so deeply. We too become angry at evil and injustice in the world, and God cares far more than we do. Jeremiah's pain (vs 19–21) reflects God's own pain, and God's cry in verse 22 confirms that fools are not people without intelligence but those who deliberately reject God.

> 'So put on sackcloth, lament and wail, for the fierce anger of the LORD has not turned away from us.'
>
> **Jeremiah 4:8**

RESPOND

If you can, look at a newspaper or news website. What makes you sad? Angry? Bring it to the God who cares and who will ultimately deal with all evil and injustice.

Bible in a year: Ruth 3,4; Psalm 45

Saturday 23 April
Jeremiah 5:1–19

Epic fail

PREPARE

Spend a few moments quietly giving to God anything which might distract your thoughts and asking for a sensitivity to what he wants to say to you today.

READ

Jeremiah 5:1–19

EXPLORE

God still looks for a way to avoid judgement, for just one person who will focus on truth (v 1), but in vain. The people no longer belong to God (v 10; see Hosea 1:9). The things which stand out are their stubbornness (v 3), complacency and self-deception (v 12), encouraged by false prophets who speak what the people want to hear (v 13). By contrast God's word gets things done (v 14). There is an ironic sense of the punishment fitting the crime (v 19).

Our first reaction is to be horrified by the behaviour of these people. How can they turn away from God, the only source of life? How can they ignore all the warnings? But our hearts have the same seeds of self-centredness and wilfulness. There will be judgement and it will start with the people of God (1 Peter 4:17).

This is a bleak picture. But there is still a chink of light, a hint of hope (v 18). Later in Jeremiah we shall meet beautiful descriptions of restoration which point to the hope we have in Jesus, who frees us from the fear of judgement (1 John 4:18) by taking it for us.

> 'Yet even in those days,' declares the LORD, 'I will not destroy you completely.'
>
> **Jeremiah 5:18**

RESPOND

Ask God to show you any areas of your life in which you are trying to run things yourself. Recommit yourself to doing things God's way and ask for his help.

Bible in a year: 1 Samuel 1–3; Mark 9

Longing for God

PREPARE
Recognise your need of God. Pray for a fresh meeting with him today.

- -

READ
Psalms 42,43

EXPLORE
What a contrast with what we have been reading in Jeremiah. The people of Judah were set on ignoring God; here is someone who longs to meet with God (v 2). The writer's situation is not completely clear. He can't get to Jerusalem to join in the Temple worship of Israel, but we are not told why. His unfulfilled longings leave him in a dark place (42:5,9,11; 43:2,5). The taunts of others make the pain worse (v 10). These notes are being written a year into the coronavirus pandemic and many are feeling the same longing to worship with others; worshipping together sustains our faith. But while the main focus here is on corporate worship, the psalm also speaks of personal longing for a deeper sense of God's presence.

Whatever the circumstances, if we are finding that God seems distant, we can be encouraged by this psalm. Yes, it may be tough and dark, and we may feel alone. We may even feel that God has deserted us. But we can, like the psalmist, hang on in the knowledge that the time will come when we can praise again – a recurring refrain in the psalm (42:5,11; 43:5). In times of darkness that may not be easy. It may even be impossible, which is why contact with other Christians is so important.

> Why, my soul, are you downcast? Why so disturbed within me? Put your hope in God, for I will yet praise him, my Saviour and my God.
>
> **Psalm 42:5,11; 43:5**

RESPOND
Pray for the worship of your church today, that it might bring a sense of joy in the presence of God.

- -

Bible in a year: 1 Samuel 4–6; Mark 10

Monday 25 April
Jeremiah 6:16–30

Back to the future

PREPARE

Think back to the time when you were first conscious of meeting with Jesus. Let your memory encourage and refresh you.

READ

Jeremiah 6:16–30

EXPLORE

Conspiracy theories abound. At the time of writing, top of the list are stolen elections and Covid vaccines that alter DNA or plant microchips. Ancient Judah had their own versions – chiefly that they would be OK whatever they did, and that God was weak and ineffective. Look at verse 14 to see what the false prophets were saying.

The antidote to the conspiracy theory is to go back to the beginning (v 16). While people rarely like to be told that things were better in the old days, which they probably weren't, there is ancient wisdom that is worth seeking out, ancient wisdom that will bring rest and freedom from judgement. What is the ancient wisdom (v 19)? It is the law of God. Three times they are told to listen or hear (vs 17,19) and listening lies at the heart of God's covenant relationship with his people then and now – God *spoke* from Sinai and still speaks. 'Listen' (NIV) is not the best translation; 'pay attention to' (ESV) is better. We are encouraged to active listening that involves obedience. But it must be genuine obedience – just going through the motions (v 20) is not enough. It may not be a popular idea, but the New Testament emphasises again and again the need for obedience (eg John 14:15).

> This is what the Lord says: 'Stand at the crossroads and look; ask for the ancient paths, ask where the good way is, and walk in it, and you will find rest for your souls.'
>
> **Jeremiah 6:16**

RESPOND

What ancient paths do you need to revisit today? Reflect on the heart of your faith and find rest.

Bible in a year: 1 Samuel 7–9; Mark 11

Misplaced trust

PREPARE

Pause to acknowledge God's place in your life. Recognise God's love for you and reaffirm your love for God.

READ

Jeremiah 7:1–29

EXPLORE

God had promised there would always be a descendant of David on the throne (2 Samuel 7:11b–16). He had chosen Jerusalem as 'his place' (Psalm 132:13,14; Deuteronomy 12:5). That's all right then! 'No, it's not!' says Jeremiah. The promises were being abused. Judah had made the Temple into a magic talisman. They were oppressing others and breaking the law (vs 6,9) and then going to worship assuming that made it OK (v 10). They believed that God would not act, but they were wrong. They were trusting in the means rather than in God himself. Things have become so bad that Jeremiah is not to pray for the people (v 16). A line has been crossed.

God's promises are not blank cheques; they come with conditions attached. Back in Exodus God promised that Israel would be his special people if they obeyed (Exodus 19:5,6); the 'if' matters. God's love for his people may persist in the face of their sin and rebellion, but the relationship can be broken. God is gracious and patient, but we cannot presume on his grace and patience. We have a part to play in maintaining the relationship. The old hymn which tells us to 'trust and obey' may sound a little trite but captures an important truth.

'... when I brought your ancestors out of Egypt ... I gave them this command: obey me, and I will be your God and you will be my people.'

Jeremiah 7:22,23

RESPOND

What might you need to do to ensure that your trust is in God alone and not in anything else? Where else might it be placed?

Bible in a year: 1 Samuel 10,11; Psalms 46,47

Wednesday 27 April
Jeremiah 7:30 – 8:7

Staying away

PREPARE
Acknowledge the holiness of God and recognise what it means to come into the presence of a holy God.

READ
Jeremiah 7:30 – 8:7

EXPLORE

In my younger days when I used to play rugby, I would sometimes come off the field caked in mud: a shower and a washing machine were called for (except that we didn't have a washing machine in those days). We can understand what it means to be filthy and need a good clean-up. That's the picture in verses 30–32, but there is a deeper dimension that is strange to us. Their sin, their idolatry and now their child sacrifice which is particularly abhorrent to God (v 31) had made the land ritually unclean. It could no longer be the Promised Land flowing with milk and honey.

The descriptions of the coming judgement are harrowing (vs 7:31 – 8:3). But the people of Judah have brought it on themselves. The tragedy is that the natural world knows how to make the right responses (v 7), but Judah has no intention of returning to God. It all seems so unnatural (v 4). That is precisely what sin is. We were made for fellowship with God – that is natural. The natural thing when we turn away is to come back (vs 4–6). But humans in every age prefer to go their own way.

'Why then have these people turned away? Why does Jerusalem always turn away? They cling to deceit; they refuse to return.'

Jeremiah 8:5

RESPOND

It's hard to know how to respond to verses like these. We feel numbed. Perhaps it is a time to pray that we might have the sensitivity to know when we need to turn afresh to God.

Bible in a year: 1 Samuel 12,13; Mark 12

Who'd be a prophet? (1)

PREPARE
Recall or read John 3:16. Thank God for his love in sending Jesus into the world.

READ
Jeremiah 8:20 – 9:11

EXPLORE

We have already seen Jeremiah's pain (4:19–21). Here it is again, but darker and more intense. It will get worse later. As he sees the sin of the people and contemplates their fate he is torn between weeping (v 1) and escaping (v 2). The opportunity has passed (v 20), there is no cure available (v 22). God has exhausted every other avenue (v 7). Any sensitive person would react as Jeremiah does. Paul has a similar reaction in Romans 9:1–3. When we respond in this way, we are reflecting the pain which God feels and which Jesus shows as he approaches Jerusalem (Luke 19:41–44). To be a prophet is not only to speak God's word but to feel God's pain.

We are not all called to be prophets as Jeremiah was, or to the sort of missionary enterprise that Paul was, but we are, as followers of Jesus, called to be his representatives in a broken world. That will mean feeling something of God's heart for the world especially as we see it in Jesus. It is easy to speak about judgement without feeling the pain, or to feel the pain and hold back from talk of judgement. But both must go alongside one another.

> Oh, that my head were a spring of water and my eyes a fountain of tears! I would weep day and night for the slain of my people.
>
> **Jeremiah 9:1**

RESPOND
Spend some time reflecting on God's heart for a broken world and for lost people. Ask him what he would have you do.

Home-made gods

PREPARE
Use a favourite song or hymn to focus on the power and majesty of God.

READ
Jeremiah 10:1–25

EXPLORE

Jeremiah has no time for idols; similar satire and ridicule can be found elsewhere in the prophets (especially Isaiah 40:18–20; 44:9–20) and in the psalms (Psalm 115:4). And God has no time for idols, as we have already seen. We see it too in the frequent commands not to make images from Exodus 20:4 onwards. The tragedy is that people readily exchange the living God for dead blocks of wood and stone.

Look at some of the contrasts. God is living (v 10); they are lifeless (v 14). God is the Creator (vs 12,16); they are man-made (vs 3,4,14). God is powerful (vs 6,12); they are weak and ineffective (v 5). See how many more you can spot.

We feel the mockery of wooden idols is spot on. But our idols are different. Anything which expresses a desire to live independently of God, anything which takes the time and energy which is due to God alone, can become an idol. We laugh at the thought of being taught by 'worthless wooden idols' (v 8). But how far are we influenced by the words of social media influencers, style gurus, media personalities? To what extent do we prefer 'gods' we can control to the God who requires our obedience?

> But the LORD is the true God; he is the living God, the eternal King.
>
> **Jeremiah 10:10**

RESPOND
Pray for those in positions of influence in our world – and for those who pay too much attention to them.

Bible in a year: 1 Samuel 16,17; Psalm 48

Who'd be a prophet? (2)

PREPARE

Have you ever faced opposition for being a Christian? What brought it about? How did it feel?

READ

Jeremiah 11:1–23

EXPLORE

Not only does Jeremiah have to face up to the pain of feeling God's heart for the world, he also has to face opposition from his contemporaries. Speaking truth to power is rarely popular, and that's what Jeremiah is called to do. The church has a similar role – and may face a similar fate.

We've already met the charge that Judah has broken covenant. Covenant is a central idea in the Old Testament. Jeremiah has in mind the covenant which God made with Israel at Sinai. Deuteronomy, which revisits material from Exodus and repeats the Ten Commandments, concludes with a list of blessings for the obedient and curses for the disobedient (Deuteronomy 28) and a covenant renewal ceremony as Israel prepared to cross the Jordan. This seems strange to us, but God is laying out the consequences of ignoring his requirements. They knew the stakes and chose to go their own way anyway.

This illustrates the impossibility of keeping the covenant requirements in our own strength. Thankfully (spoiler alert) God has other plans, as Jeremiah will reveal later. They focus on the new covenant which Jesus will introduce and which gives us a new motivating power enabling us to live in obedience.

'Obey me and do everything I command you, and you will be my people, and I will be your God.'

Jeremiah 11:4

RESPOND

Thank God for the new thing that he has done in Jesus. Ask for the strength of the Holy Spirit to enable you to live as he requires.

Bible in a year: 1 Samuel 18,19; Mark 14

Sunday 1 May
Psalm 44

Where are you, God?

PREPARE

Is your faith strong today or are you struggling a bit? Invite God to speak to you.

READ

Psalm 44

EXPLORE

Psalms 42 and 43 spoke of a longing for God. In one sense so does this psalm, but it comes from a deeper sense of confusion. In some ways it reflects the feelings of Jeremiah, except that Jeremiah saw the approaching disaster as the just punishment of God; here there is a sense of injustice and undeserved suffering. In that sense it is closer to Job. Once God was with them (vs 1–8), but no longer (vs 9–16), despite their faithfulness (vs 17,18); this led to confusion (vs 19–25) and desperate prayer (v 25).

Most Christians experience times like this. Inexplicable suffering comes our way and God seems not to provide any answers. First, remember that however hard it may be in the depths of our pain and confusion, we can, like the psalmist, be confident of the ultimate reality of God's unfailing love (v 26); the Hebrew word carries ideas of the covenant and God's total commitment to us.

Secondly, see how Paul picks up verse 22 in Romans 8:36, emphasising again that God's love is unconquerable. Sometimes these things are simply the result of living in a broken world. As Derek Kidner puts it, '... suffering may be a battle-scar rather than a punishment; the price of loyalty in a world which is at war with God'.*

Rise up and help us; rescue us because of your unfailing love.

Psalm 44:26

RESPOND

Adapt verse 26 as a prayer for any you know who are struggling to understand their suffering.

*Derek Kidner, *Psalms 1–72* (Tyndale Old Testament Commentaries), p170

Bible in a year: 1 Samuel 20–22; Mark 15

Running with horses

Jeremiah's ministry as a prophet spanned almost 40 years. These were extremely turbulent years for God's people.

King Josiah and Jeremiah were contemporaries. Reform was attempted following the discovery of the Book of the Law (2 Kings 22,23; 2 Chronicles 34).

About the writer
Elaine Duncan

Elaine is CEO of the Scottish Bible Society. She is passionate about people growing in their relationship with God through encountering him in his Word.

However, God's people persisted in going their own way and rebelling against God. Jeremiah's calling as a prophet was not an easy one. He had hard messages to bring to a rebellious people.

The chapters we are focusing on for the next week are full of oracles of doom! God has made it clear in the covenant given to Moses that if his people do not obey and follow his commands then judgement will come (Deuteronomy 28:15–68).

Jeremiah's own relationship with God was a robustly honest one. He complains and argues with God (for example 12:1–4); he pleads with God on behalf of the nation (for example 14:19–22); he doesn't give up when the going gets tough (17:14–18) or when his own life is threatened (12:6).

Is there any hope to be found in what we will read this week? Yes! God's judgement is real and always has a purpose. He is trying to get the attention of his people (13:15) in order that they will repent and turn back to him. Restoration of covenantal relationship is always the goal.

God's ultimate answer to human sin and rebellion was to send his Son Jesus as the Saviour of the world.

Monday 2 May
Jeremiah 12:1–17

Running with horses!

PREPARE
Have there been times when you have slipped into self-pity? What helped you climb out of that particular pit?

READ
Jeremiah 12:1–17

EXPLORE
Jeremiah has had to take a hard message to God's people. It has not gone down well, to the extent that people from his own town are now plotting against him (11:18). Before pouring out his heart and his complaint to God, he begins with a true statement about God: 'You are always righteous, Lord' (12:1).

What a great model to follow! We can be totally honest with God in prayer and tell him everything that is on our mind and what is troubling us – which is exactly what Jeremiah does. But it's always helpful to begin such a prayer with an acknowledgement of an aspect of God's character. This begins to get our focus in the right place.

God's call on Jeremiah's life was a tough one. He will not allow Jeremiah to wallow in self-pity (v 5) and even reveals that things will get worse as his own family turn against him (v 6). God's response to Jeremiah's 'Why?' includes the judgement that comes when God's people reject him. And yet, compassion and restoration are promised when people turn back to God (v 15).

> 'If you have raced with men on foot and they have worn you out, how can you compete with horses?'
>
> **Jeremiah 12:5**

RESPOND
Jeremiah was called to draw people back to God. It was going to be a long, hard struggle. We are called to introduce people to Jesus. That can be a long, hard struggle too. Are we ready to compete with horses?

Bible in a year: 1 Samuel 23,24; Mark 16

Who is weeping?

PREPARE
As you pray for people around you to become followers of Jesus, are there any for whom you weep?

READ
Jeremiah 13:1–27

EXPLORE
God asks Jeremiah to do something dramatic. Different terms are used for the cloth: a belt; a loincloth; a girdle. Its significance is described in verse 11: it represents something that binds and brings glory. The drama of the cloth being hidden in the river and left a while, only then to be found to be useless (vs 3–7), is a stark message of judgement from God about his people (vs 8–11).

Pride seems to be the main problem. God's people are failing to listen to him. Their purpose was to be bound to God in a covenant relationship and bring him glory. However, their stubborn refusal to listen means God will give them over to their own desires and passions (vs 12–14).

Words of judgement are always hard to hear. Is there any hint of the tone of voice being used? There is certainly a strong note of warning: it does not need to be like this; do not be arrogant (v 15). There is also sadness. Jeremiah is often referred to as the weeping prophet (v 17). He speaks God's message from a tender heart. Maybe God is weeping too. 'For I take no pleasure in the death of anyone, declares the Sovereign LORD. Repent and live!' (Ezekiel 18:32).

'If you do not listen, I will weep in secret because of your pride; my eyes will weep bitterly, overflowing with tears, because the LORD's flock will be taken captive.'

Jeremiah 13:17

RESPOND
Lord God, help us to heed your warning and to hear your heart of love that calls us to be bound to you, bringing you glory.

Bible in a year: 1 Samuel 25,26; Psalm 49

Wednesday 4 May
Jeremiah 14:1–22

'Peace, peace...'

PREPARE

Have you ever been hoodwinked into thinking all was well when it wasn't? How did that make you feel?

READ

Jeremiah 14:1–22

EXPLORE

Warnings against false prophets and teachers is a recurring theme throughout Scripture. It is also a recurring theme for Jeremiah. Here in chapter 14, he tells God how hard it is for him to convey the message of judgement because other prophets keep telling the people, 'You will not see the sword or suffer famine. Indeed, I will give you lasting peace in this place' (v 13).

God is clear that these prophets are speaking lies and that he did not send or appoint them (v 14). It is hard for Jeremiah to be a lone voice speaking truth from God. This is part of the challenge of his calling.

How do we discern the voice of God today, in among the myriad of voices clamouring for our attention? The New Testament warns us that there will be false teachers within the church (for example, Acts 20:28–31). We need to keep reading the Bible and asking the Holy Spirit to show us the truth. We need to pray for those who teach the Bible, that they will be faithful to God's message.

God's message is tough but clear. The people do not want to hear it and they have plenty of people around them telling them 'what their itching ears want to hear' (2 Timothy 4:3).

'Peace, peace,' they say, when there is no peace.

Jeremiah 6:14

RESPOND

Lord God, help us to hear you speak, even when your message to us is tough and challenging.

Bible in a year: 1 Samuel 27,28; 1 Corinthians 1

The devastating effect of sin

PREPARE

Spend a few moments quietly assessing the ways in which you have rejected God's lordship over your life in recent days. Repent and pray for his mercy.

READ

Jeremiah 15:1–21

EXPLORE

It is never easy to read of God's judgement. What is reassuring is that his judgement is not arbitrary or capricious. We are given freedom by God to make our own choices, but those choices have consequences. This is one of the key things that parents seek to teach their children. God's people have consistently rejected him, and they are now facing his judgement (vs 1–9).

Jesus expresses a similar thought with an ache in his heart: 'Jerusalem, Jerusalem … how often I have longed to gather your children together … and you were not willing' (Matthew 23:37).

Jeremiah, as a faithful prophet, has prayed and pleaded for God's mercy on the people of Judah (14:7–9,19–22). We are called to do the same and pray for those around us who are not yet Christians. However, Judah's sin and rejection of God is so deep and so persistent that judgement is going to come (vs 6–9). There have been many warnings and opportunities for repentance (13:15–27), but all have been ignored.

Jeremiah continues to bring his complaints to God (vs 10–18) and is given a personal promise (vs 19–21). He never gives up being faithful to his hard call and we should never give up praying for those who resist God's call on their lives.

'You have rejected me,' declares the Lord. 'You keep on backsliding. So I will reach out and destroy you; I am tired of holding back.'

Jeremiah 15:6

RESPOND

Pray for five people you know who have not yet softened their heart towards Jesus.

Bible in a year: 1 Samuel 29–31; 1 Corinthians 2

Friday 6 May
Jeremiah 16:1–21

Glimmers of hope

PREPARE

Consider the ways in which your church community is seeking to communicate the gospel.

READ

Jeremiah 16:1–21

EXPLORE

There are times when God asks his prophets to live out the message he is seeking to communicate to his people: Hosea, Isaiah and Ezekiel were all asked to do things at great personal cost (Hosea 1; Isaiah 20; Ezekiel 24:15–24). It is the same for Jeremiah as he is asked to forgo the gift of wife and children to show what life will be like under God's judgement.

God's determination to get his message heard and understood at times requires personal sacrifice for his messengers. God coming to live as a human in the person of his Son, the Lord Jesus, is the supreme example of his commitment to have his message of love and grace towards people heard loud and clear.

God's judgement has a purpose (vs 14,15). Restoration is the goal for the people of Judah and one day it will be reported as significantly as the Exodus from Egypt. Jeremiah is inspired by this glimmer of hope and sees that a day is coming when the nations will turn to the living God (v 19).

If only God's people will recognise again that he is the Lord, the God of power and might (v 21) and that they will turn to him in repentance and faith. This is the way to life.

> 'Therefore I will teach them – this time I will teach them my power and might. Then they will know that my name is the LORD.'

Jeremiah 16:21

RESPOND

Ask the Lord to show you how you might bring a message of hope in your community. It may involve some personal sacrifice.

Bible in a year: 2 Samuel 1,2; Psalm 50

A matter of trust

PREPARE

Are there areas of your life where you find it hard to trust God fully? Ask him to draw you into a deeper, more trusting relationship with him today.

READ

Jeremiah 17:1–27

EXPLORE

Judah's sin and rebellion is deep-seated, and God continues to warn them of all they are losing because of their rejection of him (vs 1–6). The Lord lays out clearly that there are two ways to live: with God or without God. One way leads to life, the other to death. Moses presents this clearly to the Israelites: '... I have set before you life and death, blessings and curses. Now choose life...' (Deuteronomy 30:19,20).

The picture of the tree planted by the river in verse 8 is picked up in Psalm 1 which also carries the 'two ways to live' theme. The focus here is on trusting the Lord. This is a strong relational term. The best of our human relationships are built on trust. God can be trusted to the utmost.

The verses about keeping the Sabbath holy (vs 19–27) also relate to how much we trust God. The Sabbath was given as a reminder that we humans do not run the world. We can take a break from our normal activities to pause and rest. We focus on God, his goodness and faithfulness. One day in every seven, we remind ourselves who is in control. We recalibrate our deceitful hearts to the one who has made us and who loves us.

'But blessed is the one who trusts in the LORD, whose confidence is in him. They will be like a tree planted by the water...'
Jeremiah 17:7,8

RESPOND

Choose life and renew your trust in the Lord.

Bible in a year: 2 Samuel 3–5; 1 Corinthians 3

Sunday 8 May
Psalm 45

A royal wedding

PREPARE

Recall the weddings you have attended. Pray for those couples who have stayed together and for those who have separated.

READ

Psalm 45

EXPLORE

It is perhaps surprising to come across a psalm celebrating a royal wedding. The life of the king was important in the nation of Israel.

The psalm reminds the king of his responsibility as God's appointed and anointed leader (vs 2,6,7) and of the need to reign with truth, humility and justice (v 4). The king's bride is also addressed (vs 10–15). She is reminded of the need for all other relationships to be realigned as a new family is formed through marriage (v 10; see Genesis 2:24). The gift of children is expected and celebrated (vs 16,17).

I am writing this as the news of the death of HRH Prince Philip, the Duke of Edinburgh has been announced. He was married to Her Majesty, the Queen, for 73 years. What a good, long royal marriage! The writer to the Hebrews quotes verses 6 and 7 of this

psalm (Hebrews 1:8,9). But however good a human monarch may be, they will always fall short of perfection. In God's great plan of salvation, he will send his Son as the King of kings and in the fullness of time his people, the church, will be the King's bride (Revelation 19:7,8).

> Let the king be enthralled by your beauty; honour him for he is your lord.
>
> **Psalm 45:11**

RESPOND

'Lord Jesus, thank you that you are my Lord and King. Help me to live out this reality in beauty and honour, that others may come to know you. Amen.'

Bible in a year: 2 Samuel 6,7; 1 Corinthians 4

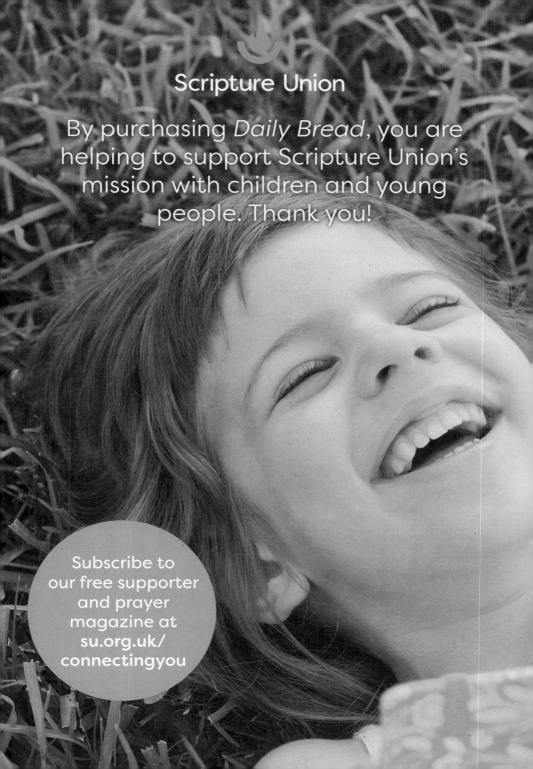

Scripture Union

By purchasing *Daily Bread*, you are helping to support Scripture Union's mission with children and young people. Thank you!

Subscribe to our free supporter and prayer magazine at su.org.uk/ connectingyou

No compromise

Following on from the last issue of *Daily Bread*, we arrive at the centre of Revelation. This deeply challenging book is written for churches in the Roman province of Asia Minor on a collision course with the might of Rome. Followers of Jesus live in city states which lead the Roman world in the practice of the imperial cult, the worship of the Roman emperor. A rejection of this cult is an act of political and religious treason – there is no separation of church and state. Christians are uncomfortable outsiders: to choose to follow Christ can mean economic, political and social ostracism, even martyrdom.

A book about survival in extreme times calls for extreme language: apocalyptic language full of vivid imagery and layered symbols. This is a language of resistance where codes are used for those ruled by an oppressive power, outlining the real dangers of compromise. It's also a language that provides comfort for those longing for justice. Apocalyptic language 'draws back the curtain', revealing the reality behind apparent reality – a heavenly perspective on an earthly situation.

From Chapter 12 onward the vision is of an earthy empire that is doomed. Despite everything, John reminds his readers – and all of us – that God is still at work, powerfully acting in and through history.

The irony is that God unconventionally 'conquers' the world through weakness and suffering, through the death and resurrection of Christ, the Lamb who was slain. And the Christian community has an essential role in God's plan of salvation as a witnessing and persecuted church.

About the writer
Michele Smart

Michele is a writer and editor. She lives on Sydney's northern beaches with her husband and two kids and dog. She surfs badly.

Into the wilderness

PREPARE

Martin Niemöller, the German theologian and pastor who was imprisoned for his resistance to Hitler, was once visited by a prison chaplain who incredulously asked him why he was in prison. Niemöller retorted: 'Why are you not in prison?'*

READ

Revelation 12:1–17

EXPLORE

This chapter, at the heart of Revelation, uses dramatic imagery to depict the cosmic conflict between God and Satan, imagery that draws on the Old Testament story of the Exodus, where God powerfully saves his chosen people, leading them through the wilderness to the Promised Land. Here, a pregnant woman and her male child are pitted against the terrifying power of a red dragon (vs 1–4), representing Satan (v 9).

However, this infant represents Christ who will 'rule all the nations' (v 5). After 'war broke out in heaven' (v 7) Satan is 'hurled down' but this triumph comes through a great inversion – through 'the blood of the Lamb'. Jesus' followers, outsiders in their society, wandering in the wilderness, will also triumph through weakness and suffering (v 11). In this 'now and not yet' framework, the defeated Satan (v 12b) declares war on Christ's followers who need to 'keep God's commands and hold fast their testimony about Jesus' (v 17b).

Many of us live comfortable lives but this passage shows the reality behind reality. How does this passage help you to understand the events taking place around us?

'They triumphed over him by the blood of the Lamb and by the word of their testimony...'

Revelation 12:11

RESPOND

Pray that 'Christ, whose insistent call disturbs our settled lives,'** will give us discernment and courage to follow him whatever the cost.

*Ben Witherington 111, *Revelation: The New Cambridge Bible Commentary*, Cambridge University Press, 2003, p.187 **Janet Morley, *All Desires Known*, SPCK, 2005

Bible in a year: 2 Samuel 8–10; 1 Corinthians 5

Tuesday 10 May
Revelation 13:1–10

Whom will you worship?

PREPARE

There is no 'false advertising' in the following passage but only a sobering reminder that the choice to worship Christ can be costly.

READ

Revelation 13:1–10

EXPLORE

Flung from heaven, with power that is limited for a season, Satan now wages war on the woman's offspring – the Christian community – by unleashing the first of two beasts. Imagery from Daniel 7 is adapted to show the beast from the sea (a symbol of chaos in the Old Testament). John's readers would recognise this as the Roman Empire in all its might (vs 1,2). They are facing stark choices in deciding who they will worship.

There is overwhelming pressure on God's people because the whole earth worships both the dragon and the beast, wooed by the beast's intoxicating power (vs 4–8). What is most sobering is that there are no easy promises that believers will be spared (vs 7,10) but instead the certainty of many deaths.

In 1998 ten statues were unveiled at Westminster Abbey. Among them are victims of Nazism, communism and religious prejudice in the 20th century, including Dietrich Bonhoeffer, killed by the Nazis in 1945; and Wang Zhiming, a pastor killed during the Chinese Cultural Revolution. These individuals paid the price for following Christ.

> This calls for patient endurance and faithfulness on the part of God's people.
>
> **Revelation 13:10b**

RESPOND:

Dante in his famous poem *The Divine Comedy* presents love as the driving force in people's lives. But this love can often be defective – we can love and therefore worship the wrong thing. Revelation asks us: What or who do you place your ultimate faith in?

Bible in a year: 2 Samuel 11,12; Psalm 51

Emperor worship

PREPARE

Is it an advantage or disadvantage to be a Christian in your country? Does it give you access to power or does it disadvantage you?

READ

Revelation 13:11–18

EXPLORE

The beast from the earth represents the priests associated with the emperor cult that flourished in Asia Minor. Not only was emperor worship seen as a reflection of one's commitment to a community, but during this time large temples operated as both banks and marketplaces. Thus, there were associated privileges of economic, social and political security that came from paying homage to the emperor.

Have you ever had to make an ethical choice as a Christian that has cost you financially? In this passage those who do not bear the mark of the beast (vs 16,17) – most likely a reference to the imperial stamp on commercial documents, or the impression of the emperor's head on coins of the time – are isolated economically. They cannot 'buy or sell' (v 17) without the mark.

But this is just the beginning. The beast from the earth can also 'cause all who refused to worship the image to be killed' (v 15b).

Many scholars have related the number 666 (v 18b) to Nero but there are evil rulers from throughout history whose behaviour provides analogies. Revelation's power lies in the reminder that earthly, evil power is limited (Revelation 12:12) and that it is God who remains in control.

> '... they could not buy or sell unless they had the mark...'
> **Revelation 13:17**

RESPOND

Are you aware of a situation where you are pragmatically compromising your beliefs? Will it be costly to change your behaviour?

A different perspective

PREPARE

The Greek word for 'bear witness' is the word we have transliterated into the word 'martyr'. We are all called to 'bear witness' to Christ.* It can be costly.

READ

Revelation 14:1–5

EXPLORE

The book of Revelation has been described as 'a dramatic motion picture whose individual scenes portray the persons and actions every time from a different angle', but ultimately these provide Christians, who were under enormous pressure, with 'the visions of an alternative empire' where Christ reigns supreme.** From the terror of the beast, John reorientates his readers – we have moved from a reign of evil on earth in Chapter 13 to a heavenly perspective where instead of oppression we find liberation, and instead of suffering, celebration.

In this passage, believers are stamped with the Lamb's name (v 1), in contrast to those stamped with the beast's mark in the previous chapter (13:16,17). These believers have clearly identified with Jesus and have paid the cost ('offered as firstfruits', v 4). The number 144,000 represents completeness.

The 'new song' (v 3) with its theme of deliverance parallels the new song in Revelation 5:9. The term 'virgins' (v 4) is a metaphor for those genuine believers who have refused to compromise themselves with the world and whose character reveals them as 'blameless' (v 5).

How might a 'heavenly perspective' help you to face challenging circumstances today?

They follow the Lamb wherever he goes.

Revelation 14:4b

RESPOND

Praise Christ our Redeemer! 'To him who sits on the throne and to the Lamb be praise and honour and glory and power, for ever and ever!' (Revelation 5:13b)

*https://learn.gcs.edu/mod/page/view.php?id=4355 **Elizabeth Schussler Fiorenza, *The Book of Revelation: Justice and Judgment*, Augsburg Fortress, 1998, pp5,6.

Bible in a year: 2 Samuel 15,16; 1 Corinthians 7

A choice to make

PREPARE

People are uncomfortable with the idea of God's judgement, yet social media pile-ons and 'cancel culture' reveal a deep longing for justice and restitution. Ask God to show you any contradictions in your own attitudes to judgement.

READ

Revelation 14:6–20

EXPLORE

In this passage John assumes that everyone worships something. There is therefore a choice to be made between two stark alternatives: in Revelation's 'worship war', angels (v 6) call individuals from 'every nation, tribe, language and people' (v 6) to 'fear God and give him glory' (v 7a), pitting the worship of the Creator against the idolatrous worship of the beast (vs 9–11).

John uses two metaphors of harvest, one of grain (vs 14,15) and the other of grapes (v 19), to introduce the rest of the themes of Revelation – the gathering of God's people and the judgement that is coming to Rome. The great harvest of vs 14–16 refers to the salvation of people from every nation (Zechariah 2:11; Isaiah 49:6; Jeremiah 16:19), while the trampling of the grapes of wrath in verses 17–20 depicts God's judgement on his enemies. John alludes to the certain doom that will come to an empire that appears as all-powerful. Rome, as 'Babylon the Great', will inevitably fall (v 8).

> 'Fear God and give him glory ... Worship him who made the heavens, the earth, the sea and the springs of water.'
>
> **Revelation 14:7**

RESPOND

At the end of Revelation 13, it almost seemed like Satan and the antichrist might win, but Revelation 14 shows who is really triumphant, powerful and in control: God, his Messiah and his people. Praise him for that.

Bible in a year: 2 Samuel 17,18; Psalms 52–54

Saturday 14 May
Revelation 15:1–8

Endurance and victory

PREPARE
'Remember Jesus of Nazareth, staggering on broken feet out of the tomb toward the Resurrection, bearing on his body the proud insignia of the defeat which is victory.'* Picture the scene and reflect on the cost of his achievement.

READ
Revelation 15:1–8

EXPLORE
A vision of a heavenly victory celebration is positioned between the announcement of the final set of judgements (v 1) and the unleashing of the seven bowls of God's wrath (15:5 – 16:21). The vision of God's victorious people standing beside the sea of glass with harps in hand and singing a song of praise to God and the Lamb recalls earlier worship scenes in Revelation (4:6; 5:8,9).

The worshippers represent 'those who had been victorious over the beast and its image' (15:2). The followers of Christ have defeated the beast not by wielding the beastly weapons of power and violence, but through the blood of the slaughtered Lamb and their own costly witness, even to the point of death (12:11). In this they have imitated Christ (5:5).

This final and great deliverance is good news for the whole world, bringing people from every tribe and nation to worship the true King, echoing Old Testament images of the pilgrimage of the nations to Jerusalem (Isaiah 2:2–4; 60:1–9; Zechariah 8:22).

'All nations will come and worship before you, for your righteous acts have been revealed.'

Revelation 15:4b

RESPOND
The song of verses 3 and 4 is a beautiful compilation of verses from all over the Old Testament (for example, Psalm 111:2,3; Deuteronomy 32:4; Jeremiah 10:7). Use these verses as a basis for prayer.

*Frederick Buechner, 'The Magnificent Defeat', https://thepastorsworkshop.com/sermon-quotes-on-easter/

Bible in a year: 2 Samuel 19,20; 1 Corinthians 8

Unshakeable

PREPARE
Are you feeling joyful or fearful at the moment? Shaken or unshakeable? Karl Barth once described joy as a 'defiant nevertheless'.*

READ
Psalm 46

EXPLORE
This is a psalm of defiant trust regardless of the circumstances, for someone whose world seems to be falling apart – much like the followers of Jesus in Revelation. What images show the fragility of life (vs 2,3)?

The quiet river in the City of God (v 4) appears no match for the noisy turbulence of the previous verses. And yet, like John's vision of heaven in Revelation, the psalmist pulls the curtain back to show us the reality of God, the creator of the earth who is in control: 'he lifts his voice, the earth melts' (v 6b). Ultimately God is a 'fortress' (v 7). *The Message* version translates the opening of this psalm as, 'God is a safe place to hide, ready to help when we need him. We stand fearless at the cliff-edge of doom.' Yet, standing fearless at the cliff-edge is only possible if we realise that God is with us and fighting for us (v 11). He comforts us: 'Be still, and know that I am God' (v 10).

> 'Be still, and know that I am God; I will be exalted among the nations, I will be exalted in the earth.'
>
> **Psalm 46:10**

RESPOND
Eugene Peterson writes, 'There's more to life than your little self-help enterprises ... If God is the living centre of redemption, it is essential that we be in touch with and responsive to that personal will.'** How easy are you finding it to trust God?

*Karl Barth, *The Epistle to the Philippians*, 40th anniversary edition, WJK, 2002, p120
**Eugene H. Peterson, *The Pastor: A Memoir*, HarperCollins, 2011, p225

Bible in a year: 2 Samuel 21,22; 1 Corinthians 9

Monday 16 May
Revelation 16:1–11

The death of evil

PREPARE
Recall the last news broadcast or newspaper you saw. What aspects of the evil present in our world do you most long to be defeated?

READ
Revelation 16:1–11

EXPLORE

We come to the beginning of the end – again we see adaptations of the Egyptian plagues from the Exodus. However, these judgements are directed at the followers of the beast and the judgements affect the whole earth, not just a third of it. For instance, in Revelation 8:7,8 only one-third of the earth and sea is affected, but now the whole water supply is turned to blood (vs 3,4).

In this passage God's final judgement shows the final binding and defeat of Satan and his forces – those who have revealed their true loyalty to the beast (v 5). The angels pour out the bowls of God's wrath upon the earth (v 2), the sea (v 3), the rivers (v 4) and the sun (v 8). Then the beast's kingdom is plunged into darkness (v 10).

The judgement also is an attempt to elicit repentance (vs 9b,11b). How are people's reactions to the bowl plagues like Pharaoh's reaction to the plagues of Egypt?

Martin Luther King wrote that God '… is working through history for the salvation of his children … Evil dies on the seashore, not merely because of man's endless struggle against it, but because of God's power to defeat it.'*

> 'Yes, Lord God Almighty, true and just are your judgements.'
> **Revelation 16:7b**

RESPOND
Think again about the evils you long for God to defeat and bring them to him in prayer. How might he be calling you to join him in bringing about change?

*Martin Luther King Jr, 'The Death of Evil upon the Seashore', in *Strength to Love*, Harper and Row, 1963, p64

Bible in a year: 2 Samuel 23,24; 1 Corinthians 10

'It is done!'

PREPARE
The artist Charlie Mackesy has an illustration where a boy asks his horse: 'What's the best thing you've learned about storms?' The horse replies, 'That they end.'*

READ
Revelation 16:12–21

EXPLORE
Several allusions in today's passage all contribute to the overall theme – the defeat of the followers of the beast, an end to evil and an end to the suffering of God's people. The Euphrates River (v 12) symbolises a border of the kingdom of the beast that keeps enemies out, so the drying up of the Euphrates begins the final serving of justice on the kingdom of the beast. The 'great day of God' (v 14b) is a symbol for a final defeat. The frogs represent demonic spirits releasing propaganda (v 13) in order to seduce the world to a great final battle called Armageddon (v 16). The final bowl (v 17) repeats the earthquake from the sixth seal (6:12) but also continues the plague motif of the Exodus.

It is ironic that the idea of Armageddon has so captured both religious and popular imagination since it is only mentioned this one time in the Bible. A focus on Armageddon as representing the abandonment and destruction of the world ignores the redemptive arc of Revelation – a book that points to the ultimate restoration of everything that is good: hope, renewal and the final victory of God.

'Look, I come like a thief! Blessed is the one who stays awake...'
Revelation 16:15

RESPOND
The Exodus motif used in Revelation is a powerful reminder that God has acted to save his people in the past and that he will act again. Recall times in your life when God has saved you. Thank him.

*https://shop.charliemackesy.com/item/the-best-thing-about-storms/print

Bible in a year: 1 Kings 1,2; Psalm 55

The Old Testament Prophets

The final section of our Old Testament is the collection of the writing of the prophets of Israel. There are four 'major' prophets: Isaiah, Jeremiah, Ezekiel and Daniel (Lamentations is effectively attached to Jeremiah); and then the 12 'minor' prophets (Hosea to Malachi). The words major and minor refer to the relative length of the scrolls, not their relative importance, then or now!

Who were the prophets?

The prophets wrote all of these 16 books over about four centuries towards the end of the Old Testament. (Malachi was the last one in the 400s BC.) The prophets were Jewish men from various walks of life who encountered God and were commissioned to speak for him. They were God's spokesmen during difficult times. Their task was to call God's people away from sin and back to faith in God.

We often think of the prophets as God's 'foretellers' – describing Christ's coming in the distant future.

However, the vast majority of their ministry was as God's 'forth-tellers' – communicating God's heart to the people at that time. Since the people were not very good at hearing from God, the prophets often used extreme measures to get their attention: strong language, vivid imagery, smashed pots, buried belts and even nakedness! (The people still did not listen too well.)

What was their message?

Each prophet wrote in a specific situation, and so their messages do differ. At the same time, there are some common threads between them. They often seek to convict people of sin. They will call God's people, or other nations, to repentance and faith in God. And they will announce consequences for sin, as well as offering a message of hope. These announcements were typically local and imminent, but sometimes global and ultimate.

Here are three practical suggestions to help as you read the Old Testament Prophets.

Useful resources

How to Read the Bible for All It's Worth (Fourth edition): Gordon D Fee and Douglas Stuart: Zondervan, 2014
The Bible Project: Wisdom series: https://bibleproject.com/explore/video/the-prophets/

Try to understand the historical context of the book

Books written before the exile tend to trace something of the godlessness and hard-heartedness of God's people during these centuries of decline. As the exile gets closer, Jeremiah reflects on how the divine discipline has become a soon-coming certainty. During the exile, we have Ezekiel and Daniel writing from Babylon. Then after the exile, Zechariah, Haggai and Malachi all write in the difficult days of the nation returning to the land. This return was not what they had dreamed about; there must be something more to come in the future!

There will be geographical and historical details that remain unclear to us as we read. However, the more you can understand the historical setting of a prophetic book, the more you will make sense of its content.

Get a feel for the organisation of the book as a whole

Some prophets write an orderly account that is relatively easy to follow. Habakkuk offers a unique question-and-answer format reflecting his interaction with God about injustice and judgement. Haggai recounts four messages from God given to the nation on four specific days. Jonah tells a story in four sequential scenes. Enjoy the organisation when it is clear. But don't get frustrated when things are not so obvious. Jeremiah, for instance, is notoriously hard to date as he seems to skip backwards and forwards from one section to the next. Many of the prophets are not organised by date but by theme.

Prayerfully feel the impact in your life

It can be overwhelming to try and make sense of every detail, place name, figure of speech, etc. Instead, it can be helpful to appreciate the more complex prophets like a symphony. You don't have to identify every detail in a symphony to feel the force of themes swelling and fading. So it is in the prophets. The great themes of human sin and divine judgement will rise and fall. And you will also see God's grace shining through, offering hope of deliverance and his future kingdom. Prayerfully appreciate the forceful presentation of God's heart and ask God to help you feel its force in your life.

Writer **Peter Mead**

Peter is one of the pastors at Trinity Chippenham and a mentor with Cor Deo. He teaches at Union School of Theology and at the European Leadership Forum.

A tale of two cities

About the writer
Penny Boshoff

Penny spends half the year in Dubai with her husband, Andrew, where she teaches, writes and relishes sharing the good news with people from around the world. Penny currently serves as President for SU Council (E&W).

In Revelation Jesus gives us a glimpse into the way things really are, the spiritual reality behind our physical world. And he reveals God's future plans. He knows how earthbound and limited our understanding is. He knows we need the gift of heaven's perspective so that we don't give up on him when trials arrive.

That does not mean Revelation is an easy book! Its complex mix of genres – letter, prophecy and apocalypse – requires different methods of interpretation. Apocalyptic writing is tricky for us because we are not used to it. First-century readers, however, were adept at decoding the vivid and complex imagery, poetry and symbolism of apocalyptic texts. Single words, images and numbers were loaded with meaning from Old Testament writings and contemporary Jewish apocalyptic writings as well as references to contemporary life. Sadly, there is not space to do justice to the richly layered symbolism of apocalyptic writing in each passage this week. If you wish to explore the symbolism in greater depth, I warmly recommend Ian Paul's excellent commentary.*

In this week's readings, Jesus reveals two contrasting cities. Through complex apocalyptic metaphors and symbolism, we are shown the spiritual realities that lie behind each city. There are warnings ahead… and invitations. One city is destined for total destruction, the other is destined for everlasting glory. It is not possible to be a citizen of both!

*Ian Paul, *Revelation – Tyndale New Testament Commentary*, IVP, 2018

City limits

PREPARE
Pray these words from Psalm 119: 'Open my eyes that I may see wonderful things in your law ... The unfolding of your words gives light; it gives understanding to the simple.' Amen (vs 18,130).

READ
Revelation 17:1–18

EXPLORE
In Revelation, angelic guides reveal the truth behind two cities: Babylon (chapters 17,18) and God's Holy City (chapters 21,22). Both are personified as women, but they could not be more different.

In 586 BC the Babylonians destroyed God's Temple, razed Jerusalem and exiled God's people. Thereafter, Babylon became a symbol of earthly opposition to God's presence, his rule and his people.

Here John uses 'Babylon' as shorthand for Rome, built on its seven hills (v 9) and resplendent in imperial colours (v 4). The city is supported by the beast from the Abyss (vs 3,7,8). So we are to understand that its foundations come from a place of darkness, chaos and militant opposition to God (see Revelation 13:1–9). That is why God's people had suffered (v 6) and why they still suffer. Whenever nations and institutions prioritise wealth, power, leisure and pleasure over God, they stand in opposition to God. Despite outward appearances, the spiritual reality is rotten and damaging (v 4). Thankfully, God limits the power of those who oppose him ('for one hour', v 12), he brings justice (vs 11,16,17; see also Luke 21:9,10) and he will triumph (v 14).

'The woman you saw is the great city that rules over the kings of the earth.'
Revelation 17:18

RESPOND
Use Peter's prayer (1 Peter 5:10,11) to pray for those who suffer because of opposition to God in the places where they live and work.

Bible in a year: 1 Kings 3–5; 1 Corinthians 11

Thursday 19 May
Revelation 18:1–10

Glory be to...?

PREPARE

'Not to us, Lord, not to us but to your name be the glory, because of your love and faithfulness.' (Psalm 115:1). How have you experienced God's love and faithfulness?

READ
Revelation 18:1–10

EXPLORE

There is an intriguing mix of past, present and future tenses in the judgement on Babylon, aka Rome (vs 2,6,8). When John wrote Revelation, the fall of Rome was yet to happen, but God's word of judgement is so sure and certain it is as though it has already taken place. What a comfort this must have been for those suffering from Roman exploitation.

Rome's 'greatness' was obtained by syphoning off the resources of the lands it conquered to supply Rome's elite with luxuries (v 7). Rome's offences that 'piled up to heaven' were the sins of Babel (see Genesis 11:4), Babylon and every great imperial power since that has sought glory for itself. Could this desire to be the first, the best and to bask in glory be at the heart of God's warning (v 4)? God's people are to be different. We are to seek God's glory above all.

So how do we 'come out' of the city? Maybe we start by reassessing our investment priorities: are we investing in things destined for judgement (vs 3,9) or are our priorities shaped by Jesus, our eternal treasure (see also Luke 12:32–34)? Are we investing in our own reputation or in God's glory?

'Come out of her, my people,' so that you will not share in her sins, so that you will not receive any of her plagues...
Revelation 18:4

RESPOND

Ask the Holy Spirit to grow your desire for God's honour and glory.

Bible in a year: 1 Kings 6,7; 1 Corinthians 12

Hidden humans

PREPARE

When you look at the injustice in the world, how do you pray about it? Do your prayers match what God intends to do?

READ

Revelation 18:11–24

EXPLORE

What do great cities have? Iconic buildings that celebrate commerce, culture or religion? Or perhaps efficient transport and communication networks, the systems of trade and commerce? Ancient Rome had them all! Rome's glory was built on the resources drawn from its empire. The cargo list (vs 11–13) is a Roman trade map: wood and wheat from Africa, spices, silks and precious stones from Asia, incense from Arabia, oil and precious metals from Europe. What do you make of the last item of cargo (v 13)?

The Roman historian Tacitus wrote, 'we have slaves drawn from every corner of the world in our households … and it is only by means of terror that we can hope to coerce such scum.'* When the building of 'great' empires comes at the cost of ruined human lives, then surely we are right to rejoice when God acts swiftly and decisively ('in one hour', vs 10,17,19) on behalf of the exploited and oppressed (vs 20,24).

Our attitude to God's judgement reveals what we truly care about. The merchants' fear and distress (vs 15,19) showed they cared more about accumulation of wealth and reputation (vs 11,23) than the well-being of people. When God's priorities become our priorities, we rejoice when he sets things straight.

'Rejoice, you people of God … For God has judged her with the judgement she imposed on you.'
Revelation 18:20

RESPOND

Pray for leaders of countries, cities and businesses to lead wisely and compassionately so that all people flourish.

*Tacitus, *Annals*, 14:44

Bible in a year: 1 Kings 8,9; Psalms 56,57

Saturday 21 May
Revelation 19:1–10

Order restored

PREPARE

Get ready to join heaven's song. Listen to some – or all! – of Elevation Worship's Paradoxology,* or sing the doxology, 'Praise God from whom all blessings flow'.

READ
Revelation 19:1–10

EXPLORE

Chapter 18 ended with a ruined city: dark, unpeopled, silent (18:22–24). Chapter 19 begins with an explosion of praise as heaven obeys the command (18:20) to rejoice in God's justice (vs 2,3). The destruction of 'Babylon', the symbol of human-centred opposition to God, is reason to celebrate.

The image of smoke (v 3) is not a literal eternal bonfire but a powerful apocalyptic metaphor from Isaiah 34:9,10. The meaning is clear: those who claim the glory and power that belong to God alone (vs 1,2; see also 18:7) will face God's judgement and never ever rise again.

Once human-centred rebellion has gone, all God's people (represented by the 24 elders, all his servants, a great multitude, vs 4,5,6) and creation itself (represented by the four living creatures) are free to worship God as they were originally created to do. They serve God (v 5), live under his rule (v 6) and worship him alone (v 10). But God has more in store!

He desires an intimate, committed relationship with his people (vs 7,8). He takes us, ragged Cinderella servants, and dresses us in the righteousness of Christ (see Ephesians 5:25; Colossians 1:22) so that we can be united in love with him for ever.

'Hallelujah! Salvation and glory and power belong to our God.'
Revelation 19:1

RESPOND
The church is Christ's bride. Let us rejoice, be glad and give him glory!

*https://youtu.be/GsrgkyUXnsE

Bible in a year: 1 Kings 10,11; 1 Corinthians 13

Because he is worth it

PREPARE
If someone were to ask you, 'Why do you worship God?' how would you respond?

READ
Psalm 47

EXPLORE
Our weeks are shaped and directed by people, tasks and ambitions making demands on our time. Sundays give us a chance to reset. A day to remember why we worship God. Although this psalm was written by worshippers in Israel's Temple, the call to worship is for all peoples (v 1). It is packed with reasons why we should worship God.

Which of the reasons strikes a chord with you? The fact that God is the supreme ruler, that he is totally other, holy, exalted beyond our imagining (vs 2,8,9)? Or that he acts in justice to free people from oppression (v 3)? Or maybe you are struck afresh that he has chosen you and planned good for you (v 4). The reference to Jacob, who was a liar and schemer, reminds us that God chooses to love flawed people.

God's decision to extend his love to all nations (v 9) is worth pondering. Anyone from any nation who responds in faith to the quiet prompting of God's word becomes part of the family of Abraham. They are blessed with the covenant love of God (Galatians 3:7–9)!

God reigns over the nations; God is seated on his holy throne.

Psalm 47:8

RESPOND
So many reasons to honour God! Psalm 47 calls us to wholehearted, whole body (v 1), full-voiced joyful worship. Think of one of those reasons, then sing, play an instrument, clap – whatever is appropriate – just make some noise!

Bible in a year: 1 Kings 12,13; 1 Corinthians 14

Judge and executioner

PREPARE
What comfort is there in knowing that Jesus Christ is judge of all?

. . . .

READ
Revelation 19:11–21

EXPLORE
Images and metaphors from Old Testament apocalyptic texts and Jesus' words to the churches (Revelation 2,3) are mixed and layered, like an oil painting, to create this symbolic description of Jesus Christ, the Word of God (see also John 1).

The white horse (the sign of a ruler, v 11), the many crowns (v 12) and the two names (v 16) declare Jesus' authority over all people. Verse 11 describes the kind of a ruler he is (see also 3:14). His blazing eyes (1:14; 2:18) symbolise both holiness and his penetrating insight into every human heart. The 'robe dipped in blood' and 'treading the winepress' refer to his role in executing judgement (see Isaiah 63:1–6). In total, we are to understand that Christ (v 13; John 1) is God's appointed judge and executioner (v 11). Only those who follow Jesus escape his wrath (v 14).

The graphic flesh-eating image from Ezekiel's apocalyptic writing is meant to reassure us (vs 17,18,21; see also Ezekiel 39:17–20)! It depicts God's total defeat of the forces gathered in opposition to Christ and his people (v 19).

Did you notice there is only one weapon in Christ's army (vs 15,21)? How might this be a comfort in times of trial?

> Coming out of his mouth is a sharp sword with which to strike down the nations.
> **Revelation 19:15**

RESPOND
'Everything is uncovered and laid bare before the eyes of him to whom we must give account' (Hebrews 4:13). In the light of this verse, what do you want, or need, to say to the Lord?

. . . .

Bible in a year: 1 Kings 14,15; 1 Corinthians 15

Bright hope for dark days

PREPARE

Pray this prayer from Ephesians 1:18: 'May the eyes of my heart be enlightened so that I may know the hope to which you have called me. Amen.'

READ

Revelation 20:1–6

EXPLORE

Rather than delve into the various and complex interpretations of the 'thousand years', I invite you to consider how these verses might have comforted the Christians who first read them. Remember how they faced daily opposition for holding to the message of Christ (see 2:13; 3:7–9)! It looked as though Satan (literally, the accuser) had them up against the ropes. Some had suffered greatly (v 4); some were suffering still (2:10).

Revelation never entertains the idea of an even cosmic contest between good and evil. There is no struggle. An angel is all it takes to throw Satan into prison to await trial and sentencing (vs 1–3)! How might this insight into God's complete control over events help hard-pressed believers?

Remaining true to Christ was hard then (v 4). It is hard now. Knowing God's plan for the future (vs 4,6) gave persecuted, powerless first-century Christians hope for the future and strength to endure their sufferings. For them, and for us, this clearer vision of our destination – sharing a limitless, perfected life with Christ (v 6; see 2 Corinthians 4:17) – helps us endure present troubles.

> Blessed and holy are those who share in the first resurrection. The second death has no power over them, but they will be priests of God and of Christ and will reign with him for a thousand years.

Revelation 20:6

RESPOND

Which of the truths in today's passage helps you to keep going when following Jesus is tough? Root that truth in your heart.

Bible in a year: 1 Kings 16,17; Psalms 58,59

Wednesday 25 May
Revelation 20:7–15

The ledgers

PREPARE

'Turn to me and be saved, all you ends of the earth; for I am God, and there is no other' (Isaiah 45:22). Praise God for his kindness and love in calling people to him.

READ

Revelation 20:7–15

EXPLORE

Once again Revelation shows how opposition to God is global, instigated by Satan and intent on destroying God's people (vs 8,9). But before we despair, the reference to Gog (ruler of Magog) is there to reassure us. Ezekiel prophesied that Gog's coalition of nations ranged against God's people would suffer numerous judgements including fire and burning sulphur (vs 9,10; Ezekiel 38:4–6,18–23).

Forget any ideas of a cosmic battle between equal forces. When we are hard-pressed, we need to remember that God's power is unequalled. Satan is tossed like garbage into the fire and consumed completely (v 10).

Pause at verse 11. Contemplate God's supremacy. His holiness and glory are so 'awe-ful' that creation runs away. Nevertheless, God calls every human to face him, with no exceptions (vs 12,13)!

One day, our judge will decide if our lives have reflected his holiness and glory. Romans 3:23–25 sums up our guilt and our hope. The Lamb's book of life is our only hope for life in God's new chapter (v 15; 13:8). Your name is there if you have trusted God for the gift of redemption and righteousness won by Jesus.

> Then I saw a great white throne and him who was seated on it. The earth and the heavens fled from his presence, and there was no place for them.

Revelation 20:11

RESPOND

Reflect on the verse we started with (Isaiah 45:22). Pray for the nations, for friends, family and colleagues, to believe and trust Jesus.

Bible in a year: 1 Kings 18,19; 1 Corinthians 16

Prepared for love

PREPARE

Pray for power to grasp the width, length, height and depth of Christ's love for you.

READ
Revelation 21:1–14

EXPLORE

Every one of our 14 verses is packed with beautiful truths about God, his nature and his plan. Consider verses 1, 4 and 8. God's judgement and destruction of death (20:4,14) and of everything that is not covered in the righteousness of Christ (20:15; 21:8) means that his new creation is free from suffering (v 4) and safe (the high wall symbolises security, v 12).

God's Holy City/bride contrasts starkly with the 'prostitute' city Babylon. Whereas Babylon was consumed with her own glory, God's prepared people shine with God's glory (v 11). Those who were sin-soaked and separated from God are now brought near, by God's own initiative. He prepares his people (the Holy City) in holiness (vs 2,6,10) so that we can be united for ever with the Lamb (Christ).

What do the references to relationship (vs 3,7,9) tell us about God's yearning to know us, love us and protect us? We are God's people, his children, his bride and wife. The City expresses the nature of our relationship with our Lord: it is intimate (v 9), welcoming and accessible (v 13), holy (pure as crystal, v 11) and permanent (like a precious stone, v 11).

> I saw the Holy City … coming down out of heaven from God, prepared as a bride beautifully dressed for her husband.
>
> **Revelation 21:2**

RESPOND

You are God's servant, his child, his bride. Which of these relationships do you identify with easily and which do you need to reflect on more deeply?

Bible in a year: 1 Kings 20,21; 2 Corinthians 1

Complete

PREPARE
Sing or listen to: 'Only by grace can we enter … Into your presence you call us … and now by your grace we come'.*

. . . .

READ
Revelation 21:15–27

EXPLORE
The city is 'as wide and high as it is long' – in other words a cube. The Holy of Holies in the earthly Temple was also a golden cube, the place where the presence of God rested. It was off limits except for one day a year. Even then only the high priest could enter (see Leviticus 16). In God's new creation, the atoning work of the Lamb (see Luke 23:45,46) means there is no sin (v 27) to separate the people from the holy presence of God. Ian Paul points out that the city is 'holiness on a cosmic scale'** as the footprint of the city is a 'Holy of Holies' (vs 15–17) large enough to encompass the entire Roman Empire. There is no inner court accessible to priests alone, no court of women, no court of Gentiles. The hierarchy of access to God is gone for good (v 22).

All the gems that make up the foundations (vs 18–20) correspond to the gems that represented God's people on Aaron's ephod (Exodus 28:15–21). The message is clear: all God's precious people have their place here. All who belong to the Lamb (v 27) are welcome into the very presence of God.

> I did not see a temple in the city, because the Lord God Almighty and the Lamb are its temple.
>
> **Revelation 21:22**

RESPOND
Which part of today's vision for your glorious future with God will you fix in your mind to help you endure your current difficulties? See Romans 8:18.

*Gerrit Gustafson, 1990, https://youtu.be/rrYK-jOnGm0
**Ian Paul, *Revelation – Tyndale New Testament Commentary*, IVP, 2018

. . . .

Bible in a year: 1 Kings 22; Psalms 60,61

The curse reversed

PREPARE

What do you long for? Bring those longings to the Lord. Listen to his invitation: 'Let anyone who is thirsty come to me and drink' (John 7:37).

READ

Revelation 22:1–9

EXPLORE

Do you ever finish the day acutely aware that in the busyness of the day you have forgotten God? If so, then take heart from today's passage. One day we will serve God face to face and serve him in creation as he originally intended (v 3).

The river coming from God's throne is a picture of the presence of the Holy Spirit (see also John 7:37–39) giving abundant life to everyone and everything in the city (vs 1–3; Ezekiel 47:1–11). John's readers knew about crop failure due to irregular water flows in their hot climate. This picture of continuous provision and year-round fruitfulness is the first sign of the reversal of the curse in Genesis (Genesis 3:17–19).

The next sign is the healing of relationships between peoples (v 2; see Genesis 3:16). The Holy Spirit will continually empower us to obey God's rule in our communal life (v 2). The final sign is a fully restored relationship between God and humans (v 4). Today we may struggle to understand what God wants and struggle to obey. In his new creation he will be everything we long for and we will know how to serve him because he will guide us (v 5).

> Then the angel showed me the river of the water of life, as clear as crystal, flowing from the throne of God and of the Lamb down the middle of the great street of the city.

Revelation 22:1

RESPOND

The Spirit has already begun his work. Pray Paul's prayer in Ephesians 3:16–21 for yourself, your church fellowship and the wider body of Christ.

Bible in a year: 2 Kings 1–3; 2 Corinthians 2

Home with God

PREPARE
Jot down a list of reasons why the Lord is worthy of praise. Turn your list into prayers of praise.

READ
Psalm 48

EXPLORE

Ancient Jerusalem was a typical fortified settlement, situated on the steep slopes of Mount Zion. It was not the strategic military position that made the difference but God's presence with his people (vs 2,3,7,8). Like the layers of a Russian doll, the city surrounded the Temple, and the Temple held the Most Holy Place which contained the Ark of the Covenant. And God had promised to live with his people, enthroned above the Ark of the Covenant (see also Exodus 25:22; Numbers 7:89). God's presence brought security (v 8) and delight (v 9).

It would have been easy to sing this song when God defeated their enemies (vs 4–7; 2 Kings 19:32–36). However, there was soul-searching, doubt and mourning when the city and Temple were later destroyed. How were God's people to make sense of verses 8, 9, 10 and 14 when they stood among the ruins? How do we keep hold of the truths of God's love and righteousness (vs 9,10) when life crumbles around us? Maybe Revelation 21 holds the key: God has designed a safe city where we will live with our Great King. Where everyone (the nations, the city, the villages) will marvel at his unfailing love (v 9).

> Within your temple, O God, we meditate on your unfailing love.
>
> **Psalm 48:9**

RESPOND
Why not memorise verse 14 so that when you face tricky moments in the week ahead, you will trust him to be your 'guide even to the end'?

Coming soon

PREPARE

Jesus makes it possible for us to draw near to God (Hebrews 10:19–22). Be still and enjoy the presence of the living God.

READ

Revelation 22:10–21

EXPLORE

Jesus' word to the seven churches (1:8) crops up again (v 13), reminding us that this revelation is Jesus' gift to the church (v 16).

Jesus wants us to be sure of our destination – life with God (v 14). And if we are fixed on our relationship with him (v 17), we will be able to endure to the end. So rather than listen to the doubts of the world around us, let's listen to Jesus. He is so determined that we understand that he says it three times (vs 7,12,20).

Jesus' certain return will reverse the curse of Genesis. Adam and Eve's descendants will live with God in his garden city and eat from the tree of life (v 14). Our job is to be ready (v 12). Note the specific entry conditions (vs 14,15): only those who 'have washed their robes and made them white in the blood of the Lamb' (7:14) can enter. It is not our good works but only Christ's blood on the cross that redeems us from the consequences of sin (v 15; Ephesians 1:7) and ushers us into God's New Jerusalem (v 14).

'Let the one who is thirsty come; and let the one who wishes take the free gift of the water of life.'

Revelation 22:17

RESPOND

Just as humans need water, so God's people need his Spirit (v 17; John 7:37–39), for the Spirit prepares us for Jesus' return. Are you thirsty? Take and drink.

Bible in a year: 2 Kings 6,7; 2 Corinthians 4

"I DON'T GO TO CHURCH BUT I DO BELIEVE IN GOD"

95% of under-18s don't go to church BUT many are open to exploring faith.

Together, we can reach the 95! Find out more at **the95.org.uk**

Scripture Union

Glory into glory

About the writer
David Bracewell

On retirement, David Bracewell established 'Zoe Ministry', which aims to encourage church leaders in their task of building healthy churches. He has five grandchildren, three children and one wife. He continues to teach and preach as required and is the attentive owner of a Mazda sports car.

Preparing to write these notes I read through 2 Corinthians 1–6 fairly swiftly, not focusing on the details, but wanting to gain an overall impression. What came through was the remarkable mix of theological reflection, gritty personal experience and shrewd ethical instruction. As Paul anguishes over the wayward church at Corinth he is overwhelmed with emotion and his thought takes flight in glowing words and moving insights. His longing for reconciliation with the church leads him to profound reflection on the reconciliation that God brought through Christ on the cross which stands at the heart of the gospel.

Paul's relationship with the church in Corinth was complex and need not detain us here beyond noting that their sexual immorality, their welcoming of false teaching into the fellowship and their questioning of Paul's authority had led to a visit which caused him much pain. Withdrawing, he abandoned a second visit, instead writing a severe letter which brought a positive response leading to the writing of 2 Corinthians.

It is a deeply moving document and it is such a privilege to be studying it with you. May I suggest that you take time to read the chapters through at one go? And if you feel you haven't time, may I be cheeky and suggest you make time! It will be well rewarded, and it took me just 15 minutes!

Tuesday 31 May
2 Corinthians 1:1–11

Words of comfort

Think of a time when you experienced God's comfort. Did that help you to offer comfort to others?

READ
2 Corinthians 1:1–11

EXPLORE

Those of us of a certain age, me included, may remember the Beatles lyrics 'Speaking words of wisdom, let it be' (1970). Paul begins his letter speaking words of *comfort* – over and over again. The word has the meaning of standing alongside, giving strength. Not so much being wrapped in cotton wool, more being gently prodded. We tend to prefer cotton wool, wanting to be shielded from hardship and sheltered from difficulties. But God's comfort operates in the midst of troubles, enabling us to stand and to know his presence. The Holy Spirit is the Comforter who stands alongside us (and prods us!) (John 16:7).

Moreover, we are not the centre of the picture. Comfort flowed from God to Paul, and then from Paul to the church. There was a cascade effect, and the catalyst was suffering (v 7). In Paul's case it was not just a minor irritation but a life-threatening attack (v 8). So much so that his deliverance felt like a resurrection (v 9)!

Suffering, comfort, awareness of others: it is a life-giving sequence that God wants to develop in your life and mine... speaking words of comfort, let it be. And indeed it will be, because our God is the God of all comfort.

> For just as we share abundantly in the sufferings of Christ, so also our comfort abounds through Christ.
> **2 Corinthians 1:5**

RESPOND

Are you overwhelmed today? Pray that God will send someone alongside you and then gently prod you into getting alongside someone else.

Bible in a year: 2 Kings 8,9; Psalms 62,63

Let me explain

PREPARE

Think back to a time when someone close to you misunderstood your actions. How did you feel, and what did you do?

READ

2 Corinthians 1:12 – 2:4

EXPLORE

Those who brand Paul – and there are many – as an austere theologian can never have read this letter. A strong will certainly (v 12); a sharp mind of course (v 20). But a cold heart? Never! The Paul we meet today seems close to emotional meltdown.

The aborted visit (v 23) and the stern letter (2:3) are playing on his mind and he is desperate for the church to know the truth. He wasn't being fickle or manipulative. He just loves this wayward bunch of disciples and wants to be in fellowship with them.

The emotion is raw, but the theology is radical. The relationship has become fractured but cannot finally be broken because it flows from their mutual trust in God the Father who has rooted them in his Son Jesus, and sent his Spirit into their hearts assuring them that they belong (vs 21,22). No amount of misunderstanding can withstand this trinitarian security! If today you are feeling wounded by another Christian, recall the unity you have because you both belong to Christ. Then, while work may still be needed to mend the trust that has been broken, you will be well on the way to a joyful reunion!

For I wrote to you out of great distress and anguish of heart and with many tears, not to grieve you but to let you know the depth of my love for you.

2 Corinthians 2:4

RESPOND

'Lord, help me to make the first move *today* to mend that relationship that has been broken. Amen.'

Bible in a year: 2 Kings 10–12; 2 Corinthians 5

2 Corinthians 2:5–11

We're in this together

PREPARE

Think back to a time when someone forgave you for a hurt you had caused. How did it feel?

READ

2 Corinthians 2:5–11

EXPLORE

Paul still has the severe letter on his mind. It had worked – but not quite in the way he had intended! One purpose of the letter had been to urge the church to address an incident of serious misconduct. The person involved needed to be punished. In Paul's mind the sequence would be: punishment, forgiveness, restoration. The church hadn't got beyond punishment! They had carried out his instruction but misunderstood (or ignored?) the deeper purpose. The result was that the offender was demoralised and Satan was having a field day (v 11).

Paul says, in effect, 'Tell him that you love him, forgive him and welcome him back' (vs 7,8). And is there a hint in verse 10 that beyond forgiveness there is forgetfulness (see Psalm 103:12)? Punishment delivered without love – then and now – will only result in despair. It's a delicate balance, but if the intention shifts from restoration to revenge, all will be lost. The people involved will suffer, but so will the whole church (v 5) because we belong together. Paul had taught them that earlier (1 Corinthians 12). We really are all in this together (Romans 12:15).

If anyone has caused grief, he has not so much grieved me as he has grieved all of you to some extent – not to put it too severely.

2 Corinthians 2:5

RESPOND

We may think, 'What a terrible bunch they were in Corinth.' We mustn't! Instead let's have a clear-eyed view of our own fellowship and pray that God will fill us with love and the power to forgive.

Bible in a year: 2 Kings 13,14; 2 Corinthians 6

A rich aroma

PREPARE

Memories can be joyful or sad. What are some of the memories you have and how are they evoked?

READ

2 Corinthians 2:1–17

EXPLORE

'Wake up and smell the coffee' is a challenge often thrown out to someone who seems unaware of the significance of events going on around them. Fresh coffee, newly mown hay, sizzling bacon, or fragrance from a rose: smells have the power to catch us unawares, evoking memories, sometimes joyful, sometimes painful. They flood in, unbidden, to comfort or unsettle us.

Paul takes this idea, probably from the memory of Roman triumphal processions where incense was often burned (v 14), and applies it to our discipleship: we are an aroma that brings life (v 16). Our lives, impregnated with the presence of Christ, can evoke spiritual realities in those who meet us. They can either strengthen faith or confirm unbelief. No wonder Paul is overwhelmed with the responsibility (v 16). So am I! And you are too, I imagine.

But no need to despair. Unlike those who proclaim Christ for their own ends and profit – the Corinthian church would get the reference to the false teachers who had invaded the church (v 17) – we who serve and speak with integrity and a clear sense of being called will be led triumphantly in the way of Christ for his glory and our well-being (v 14).

> For we are to God the pleasing aroma of Christ among those who are being saved and those who are perishing.
>
> **2 Corinthians 2:15**

RESPOND

'Lord, lead me to someone today whose heart will be strangely warmed as they sense your presence in me. For Jesus' sake. Amen.'

Bible in a year: 2 Kings 15,16; Psalms 64,65

I can read you like a letter

PREPARE
If someone were to write a letter of commendation for you, what would it say?

READ
2 Corinthians 3:1–6

EXPLORE

My first vicar taught me that in the event of a dispute it is far better to see the person involved rather than write a letter. We can be grateful that on this occasion Paul didn't follow that advice, otherwise we would never have had this marvellous letter! Hovering in the background is the issue of the false teachers at Corinth who were trying to undermine Paul's ministry. They followed the customary practice of providing letters written by other churches (or possibly by themselves!) commending their work (v 1).

Paul did not need such testimony to authenticate his ministry: no character references, no framed qualifications on his office wall – just lives transformed by Jesus and indwelt by the Spirit of God (vs 2,3). He dispenses with pen and ink, instead pointing to flesh and blood people whose lives are an open letter able to be read by anyone. This approach puts the church on the spot of course.

Would people visiting Corinth 'read' them? Perhaps this bit of the letter challenged them to 'get a grip' and mend their ways.

We too have care and responsibility for others – whether a child, or partner, or friend or colleague. Are their lives, as the result of our influence, a book that others would delight to read?!

> You yourselves are our letter, written on our hearts, known and read by everyone.
>
> **2 Corinthians 3:2**

RESPOND

A transformed life is a more reliable guide than a formal reference, but when recommending someone, maybe both are needed. What would someone write in your letter of commendation?

Bible in a year: 2 Kings 17,18; 2 Corinthians 7

Glory into glory

PREPARE
Before you read today, glance in the mirror. What sort of face do you see? On this Pentecost Sunday, be ready for transformation.

READ
2 Corinthians 3:7–18

EXPLORE
As I begin to write this note I'm seized with mild panic. These verses are so rich, so deep, so glorious. Where to begin?

Glory, repeated 12 times, seems the obvious place. Glory is the self-revelation of God in all his brilliant splendour (Luke 9:29) and majestic power (Romans 6:4). That glory, veiled under Moses' ministry, now under the new covenant (v 6), shines out in the face of Jesus. But here's the thing. The glory of God on the face of Jesus is reflected on the faces of his disciples. You and me! Really? I don't know about you, but I have a long way to go.

But mercifully this transformation is a lifetime process. Day by day, inch by inch, the glory spreads as we turn our faces to the Son. And this is not a private affair. We do it together as we see on the face of the person next to us in church a glimpse of God's glory (v 18). It takes time and we must be purposeful.

In the story of the transfiguration the disciples were asleep, and it was only when they woke up that they saw the glory (Luke 9:32). Rather more prosaically, my son says to me: 'Dad, if you snooze you lose.'

And we all, who with unveiled faces contemplate the Lord's glory, are being transformed into his image with ever-increasing glory, which comes from the Lord, who is the Spirit.

2 Corinthians 3:18

RESPOND
Have another look in the mirror. Pray that the transforming light of God's Spirit will increasingly shine through you.

Bible in a year: 2 Kings 19,20; 2 Corinthians 8

Monday 6 June
2 Corinthians 4:1–6

Telling the truth

PREPARE
What 'gods' would you say blind people to the truth of Christ today?

- -

READ
2 Corinthians 4:1–6

EXPLORE
Surveys seeking to establish what people most look for in a leader consistently come up with integrity. Paul had it in spades! Unlike the false teachers at Corinth, with Paul there was no deceit, no distortion, no dissembling. Just the plain truth proclaimed 'in the sight of God' to whom he was accountable. That truth is embodied in 'the gospel that displays the glory of Christ' (v 4). At this point Paul's thought and language take flight as he focuses on the One who has captivated his heart. The One whom he serves and for whose sake he serves the church.

Jesus who is the image of God, Jesus who shines the glory of God into the lives of those who turn to him, Jesus who is Lord, Jesus whom Paul proclaims as the truth. By contrast those who choose to follow false idols find themselves consigned to darkness, blind to the glory of Jesus who is the truth

(John 3:19). It is a sobering thought. May it challenge you and me to tell the truth to all who will listen. While that truth will be incarnated in our own personality and conveyed through our own 'story', it will, at the same time, point away from ourselves revealing the glory of Jesus Christ.

> For what we preach is not ourselves, but Jesus Christ as Lord, and ourselves as your servants for Jesus' sake.
>
> **2 Corinthians 4:5**

RESPOND
'Lord, guide me to one person today with whom I can share the truth of the gospel. Amen.'

- -

Bible in a year: 2 Kings 21,22; 2 Corinthians 9

Down but not out

PREPARE

If today life seems a challenge, read on and take heart. You are in good company.

....

READ

2 Corinthians 4:7–12

EXPLORE

Things are never straightforward with Paul. He gives the Corinthians a glimpse of how it is for him. Fragile, like a clay pot, bruised and battered by others, experiencing a sense of dying. But, he says, the pot is full of treasure. Knocked down, he is never 'out for the count'. Experiencing a sense of dying, he is able to bring life to others. What a man! Catch the mood of Paul's words as he recalls the pressure and perplexity, the persecution and pain that had been his lot.

This is light years away from the notion which can work its way into our consciousness that our following of Christ will give us a life of ease and plenty. It's so easy to develop a 'L'Oreal' spirituality: 'because you're worth it'! But it is not so. Ease and plenty are not our destiny as disciples. We are more likely to encounter threat and danger. But with it the sheer exhilaration of following

Jesus. And this fragile, unprepossessing clay pot, despite all that has conspired to destroy it, remains unbroken, still holding the priceless treasure of the gospel (v 7).

> We always carry around in our body the death of Jesus, so that the life of Jesus may also be revealed in our body.

2 Corinthians 4:10

RESPOND

We must expect wounds, for we follow a wounded Lord. If this is true, how will that affect the way you live today?

....

Bible in a year: 2 Kings 23–25; Psalms 66,67

Don't lose heart

PREPARE

If today you are tempted to be disheartened, try to step back from your immediate circumstances and look at the bigger picture.

READ

2 Corinthians 4:13–18

EXPLORE

When I was discussing some minor ailment with a friend recently, he said to me, 'Well, we are all outwardly wasting away.' Not altogether helpful, but undoubtedly true! Paul draws a series of contrasts here (vs 16–18). Outwardly wasting away, but inwardly being renewed; brief trials but lasting glory; visible things that are temporary, but unseen things that are eternal. Living with these paradoxes, Paul is neither perplexed nor frustrated, but emboldened (3:12; 4:1).

The key issue is the towering truth of the resurrection. I happen to be writing this note on Easter Sunday. 'The Lord is risen! He is risen indeed!' Here and now we are risen with Christ (Colossians 3:1) and one day, beyond 'the changes and chances of this fleeting world', we will stand in his presence (v 14). This changes everything.

Moreover, this secure future with Christ flows back into our present trials and tribulations, putting them into perspective and firing us to speak life-changing truth, and display amazing grace for the good of those around us and to the glory of God (vs 13,15). Are you feeling a bit less disheartened?

> Therefore we do not lose heart. Though outwardly we are wasting away, yet inwardly we are being renewed day by day.
>
> **2 Corinthians 4:16**

RESPOND

'Lo, Jesus meets us, risen from the tomb; / Lovingly he greets us, scatters fear and gloom … / Thine be the glory, risen, conqu'ring Son …' (Edmond Budry, 1854–1932).

Bible in a year: 1 Chronicles 1–3; 2 Corinthians 10

Head in the clouds?

PREPARE

It has been said that a person is not really ready to live until she or he is ready to die. What do you think?

READ

2 Corinthians 5:1–10

EXPLORE

'You are so heavenly minded, you're no earthly use.' Not infrequently I have this spoken over me, having neglected some basic domestic duty because 'my head was in the clouds'! Perhaps you can identify with me.

Paul's head (and heart) are most certainly in the clouds as he passionately expresses his desire to depart this life and be with Christ. His passion for what is to come puts to shame my own easy satisfaction with my material existence.

But, of course, it is not a question of either/or. Paul explains that the Spirit of God is given to whet his appetite for the life to come and at the same time to focus his mind on pleasing God in Corinth! So it is for us. The more our heads are in the clouds the greater should be our desire to please God on earth, here and now. Today. With his head so in the clouds, can he focus on the here and now? Well, yes. There is the small matter of having to give account of his life before the judgement seat of Christ. It is in fact a very large matter and should concentrate our minds not in fear, but in joyful abandonment to please God every day.

> So we make it our goal to please him, whether we are at home in the body or away from it.
>
> **2 Corinthians 5:9**

RESPOND

'Lord, help me today to live with my head in the clouds and my feet on the ground. Amen.'

Bible in a year: 1 Chronicles 4–6; 2 Corinthians 11

Friday 10 June
2 Corinthians 5:11 – 6:2

Life is for living

PREPARE

Do you feel you are living life to the full, or is it all a bit of an effort? Be honest! Ask God to inspire you afresh as you read his Word today.

READ

2 Corinthians 5:11 – 6:2

EXPLORE

I've just been listening to a podcast in which a doctor and a psychotherapist were discussing 'How to create the life you were born to live'. It was a powerful and moving piece, but turning from it to today's reading I saw that their proposal could only find fulfilment in the Christian gospel. We cannot create 'the life we were born to live', and can only receive it as a gift coming to us through the death and resurrection of Jesus. Through the cross we are reconciled to God and become 'a new creation' as our physical lives are invaded by God's eternal life (vs 17,18).

Only then can we begin to understand who we are and who we are meant to be, and only then will we, like Paul, be compelled to proclaim far and wide the liberating truth that in Christ all people can live the life they were born to live (v 14).

Such good news is given to share. In a world where people long for meaning, what are we waiting for? After all, 'Now is the day of salvation' (6:2).

> Therefore, if anyone is in Christ, the new creation has come: the old has gone, the new is here!

2 Corinthians 5:17

RESPOND

Read this amazing passage again slowly and thank God for the reconciliation which is both a gift and a mission. How might you respond?

Bible in a year: 1 Chronicles 7–10; Psalm 68

The cost of discipleship

PREPARE
Is your love for Christ and your passion to serve him stronger than when you first believed?

READ
2 Corinthians 6:3–13

EXPLORE
In the final verses of today's reading (vs 11–13), Paul abandons any pretence of restraint as he pours out his feelings for the Corinthian Christians. It's as though he is saying, 'My dear children in Christ, I'm writing to explain how much I love you all, and how I long that you will feel the same.' In these verses there is a key to unlocking the whole epistle. This renowned theologian, church planter, preacher, writer, missionary and foremost of apostles is a vulnerable human being who – like us – longs to love and be loved!

However, this is not just about Paul's personal feelings. What he really wants the Corinthians to grasp and experience is the sheer exhilaration of a life abandoned to Christ. He wants them to shake off their petty squabbles and their sad addiction to power. To exchange the bleak landscape of church politics for what he calls elsewhere 'the freedom and glory of the children of God' (Romans 8:21). Doesn't your heart thrill at such a proposed escape?

The recounting of that abandonment is overwhelming as Paul's words pour out, coming to a climactic conclusion in 'having nothing, and yet possessing everything' (v 10). There is a similar outpouring later in the letter as he describes the cost of discipleship (11:21–29). As I read his words, I am chastened and inspired in equal measure. What about you?

> We have spoken freely to you, Corinthians, and opened wide our hearts to you.
>
> **2 Corinthians 6:11**

RESPOND
'Lord, rekindle in me today the fire of your love. Amen.'

Bible in a year: 1 Chronicles 11–14; 2 Corinthians 12

You can't take it with you

PREPARE
There's more to life than having everything. What do you think?

. . . .

READ
Psalm 49

EXPLORE
If ever there was a passage of Scripture that speaks to our consumerist culture, this is it. Wealth, property, honour – nothing escapes the final enemy. And we are all in the same boat – rich and poor, high and low, foolish and wise, all are destined to perish (vs 5–12). The psalmist has such a moment of clarity about this that he wants to shout it from the rooftops (v 1).

It's a grim message! Surely there must be a better way to live. Indeed, there is. The foolishness of materialism is not in the desire to possess, but in the capacity of material things to give their owner the illusion of immortality. Instead, the psalmist remembers God, who alone can rescue and redeem, to whom we are precious and who longs to draw us to himself (v 15).

He can break the fascination of things temporal, and rescue us, bringing us to reality. And beyond that beckoning grave there is a hint of final rescue not fully developed here (see also Daniel 12:2,3) – 'God will redeem me' (v 15). For that we need an empty tomb. Jesus said, 'I am the resurrection and the life. The one who believes in me will live, even though they die' (John 11:25).

> Do not be overawed when others grow rich, when the splendour of their houses increases.
> **Psalm 49:16**

RESPOND
George Bernard Shaw said that death is the ultimate statistic: 'one out of one dies'. So, thank God for the sane and bracing truth of the resurrection.

. . . .

Bible in a year: 1 Chronicles 15,16; 2 Corinthians 13

Chalk and cheese

PREPARE

What does the word 'holiness' conjure up in your mind? Ask God to help you understand more about what it means to be holy.

READ

2 Corinthians 6:14 – 7:1

EXPLORE

Day by day the challenge of discipleship is to become what we are – sons and daughters of God (v 18). And we are a new creation in Christ in which our old life of self-reliance is a past and fading memory (2 Corinthians 5:17). Paul lists a number of chalk-and-cheese scenarios (vs 14–16) which mark the newness of our life in Christ.

So, it makes no sense to keep reverting to the way of life we have left behind. Instead, we should be offering a lasting alternative to the secular dream world that so many inhabit. We are to be separated from all that opposes God's will and be set apart for God's service (v 17). We are to be holy before God, not holier-than-thou before other people (v 1). As we come closer to God, so we are also drawn deeper into the world he died to redeem.

These verses conclude the section of the letter that began at 2:14: 'Thanks be to God...' It's been a humbling but triumphant journey as God has led Paul, and us, into closer fellowship with his Son, and deeper communion with the world he died to reconcile. Thank you for joining me on the ride!

Therefore, since we have these promises, dear friends, let us purify ourselves from everything that contaminates body and spirit, perfecting holiness out of reverence for God.

2 Corinthians 7:1

RESPOND

If you can, take time to read these six chapters again and marvel at the sheer wonder of our reconciliation to God: Father, Son and Holy Spirit.

Bible in a year: 1 Chronicles 17,18; Galatians 1

Whose reputation?

Paul had planted the church in the Greek city of Corinth on his second missionary journey (Acts 18). The problems which arose in a church struggling to live out Christian values in a pagan world had multiplied as the church fell under the spell of false teachers (as we've begun to see in the last week or so). We cannot be sure of the details of their teaching, but they seem to have been held in high esteem. In response to the reports he receives from Corinth, Paul writes letters, only two of which survive in our Bibles.

The issues Paul addresses in 1 and 2 Corinthians are familiar to twenty-first-century Christians, and Paul's response has much to teach us about living distinctive Christian lives, both as individuals and as church communities in the midst of secular society today.

Our section here begins with references to another letter in which Paul had taken the Corinthians to task for tolerating sinful behaviour in their midst (7:8). How have they responded? He then moves on to the need for God's people to share their resources and lays down principles of Christian giving.

Paul has to respond to attacks made on his authority by the 'super-apostles' who have gained undeserved respect in Corinth, much of it by denigrating Paul. We see Paul's true priorities, as, refusing to promote himself, he focuses on his own weakness and God's grace.

Donald Carson writes: 'Here is the heart of the true apostle, a Christian so steeped in radical discipleship and firm self-discipline that his every care is for the people he serves, not for his own reputation.'*

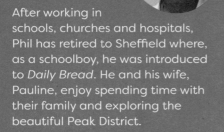

About the writer
Phil Winn

After working in schools, churches and hospitals, Phil has retired to Sheffield where, as a schoolboy, he was introduced to *Daily Bread*. He and his wife, Pauline, enjoy spending time with their family and exploring the beautiful Peak District.

*D.A. Carson, *From Triumphalism to Maturity*, Paternoster Press, 1996, p180

To whom it may concern

PREPARE
Ask God to show you an area of your life that he would like to change.

....

READ
2 Corinthians 7:2–16

EXPLORE
Have you ever written a letter, or sent an email, then regretted it? Perhaps you said things you should not have; maybe you could have phrased things better. We live in a world of instant communication. Imagine what it was like when letters were delivered by hand and travel was slow. Receiving a response could take a long time.

Paul had written another letter after the one we know as 1 Corinthians, to the church he had founded in Corinth. In it he had criticised their behaviour and called for change. As he was travelling around Macedonia (Acts 20:1–4), Paul is met by his friend Titus, who had delivered the stern letter. How had the church reacted to the criticisms it contained? Titus brought good news; the stern letter had had a good reception and the Corinthians acknowledged their mistake (v 7). How do you react if someone points out one of your faults? Denial? Anger?

Self-justification? Or do you admit the problem and determine to change?

Paul contrasts 'godly sorrow' with 'worldly sorrow' (v 10). The former results in determination to live in a way which pleases God; the latter may be characterised by regret, but falls short of a change of life. Just as Paul had hoped, the Corinthians had impressed Titus with their readiness to put things right; he now writes to encourage and further challenge them.

> Godly sorrow brings repentance that leads to salvation and leaves no regret, but worldly sorrow brings death.
>
> **2 Corinthians 7:10**

RESPOND
Could you encourage someone with a letter, card or email today?

....

Bible in a year: 1 Chronicles 19–21; Psalm 69

Wednesday 15 June
2 Corinthians 8:1–15

Sharing resources

PREPARE

Spend some time thanking God for all the good things he has given you.

READ

2 Corinthians 8:1–15

EXPLORE

I remember being challenged by a sermon, many years ago, on the Lord's Prayer. When she reached 'Give us this day our daily bread', the preacher pointed out that God could use those of us in the rich West to answer the prayer of less affluent Christians. One of the most exciting things about being a Christian is that we are part of a worldwide family; if one member is in need, the others help.

Paul reminds his readers that, as he travelled, he was making a collection on behalf of the impoverished Christians in Jerusalem (see 1 Corinthians 16:1–4). The congregations in Macedonia, from where he was writing, had responded generously to the appeal. Will the Corinthians be similarly open-handed in their response?

Christian giving cannot be compelled; it must be a generous response to the grace of God shown in Christ's self-giving love (v 9). Like the Corinthians, we need, from time to time, to review our giving. When did you last review yours? Paul reminds his readers (v 15) of God's miraculous provision of manna for his people in the wilderness; there was enough for all, but it was not to be hoarded (see Exodus 16:18).

> At the present time your plenty will supply what they need, so that in turn their plenty will supply what you need.
>
> **2 Corinthians 8:14**

RESPOND

'Thou who art love beyond all telling … Emmanuel, within us dwelling, / Make us what thou wouldst have us be … Saviour and King, we worship thee.'*

*Frank Houghton (1894–1972), from the hymn, 'Thou Who Wast Rich Beyond All Splendour'

Bible in a year: 1 Chronicles 22,23; Galatians 2

Personal recommendation

PREPARE

Reflect on these words: 'A good name is more desirable than great riches; to be esteemed is better than silver or gold' (Proverbs 22:1).

READ

2 Corinthians 8:16–24

EXPLORE

Private companies and public bodies recognise the importance of 'reputation management', sometimes paying PR companies large sums to ensure that bad news stories are suppressed, and good news promoted. Here, Paul vouches for the good reputation of his colleagues and of the church to whom he writes.

What are the best qualities of the church you belong to? Do you tell others of its strength? Despite all its shortcomings, Paul is proud of the church he founded in Corinth and wants Titus and his companions to be impressed by their generosity (v 24).

Paul had previously asked the Corinthians to start a collection for the church in Jerusalem (1 Corinthians 16:4) and now is sending Titus, whom the Corinthians already know, and two others to collect the offering. As he expects the church to be liberal (v 20),

it is important to choose such people wisely, so that money is not only handled well, but is seen to be handled well.

Paul is enthusiastic in recommending the messengers he is sending to Corinth. Titus' companions are 'the brother who is praised by all the churches for his service to the gospel' (v 18) and 'our brother who has often proved to us in many ways that he is zealous' (v 22). What would people say about you?

Therefore show these men the proof of your love and the reason for our pride in you, so that the churches can see it.

2 Corinthians 8:24

RESPOND

Who could you encourage today by telling them how well they reflect God's goodness?

Friday 17 June

2 Corinthians 9:1–15

Generous giving

PREPARE

Ask God to show you how to share what you have in order to help others.

READ

2 Corinthians 9:1–15

EXPLORE

In his hometown of Leeds, Robert Arthington (1823–1900) was known as the 'Miser of Headingley'. He had inherited a fortune but lived frugally. Unknown to his neighbours, he was using his wealth to transform thousands of lives by funding mission stations, clinics, ships and many other projects to spread the good news of Jesus.*

Although we may not have a fortune at our disposal, we all have the opportunity not only to meet the needs of others, but to enable them to give thanks to God (v 12). Have you experienced the blessing of being able to help others (Proverbs 22:9)?

Summing up his plea for funds on behalf of the impoverished Christians in Jerusalem, Paul reminds the Corinthians that they are privileged to work with a generous God. As God supplies our needs, we can help meet the needs of others.

The principle of sowing generously and reaping generously has been misused in 'prosperity gospel' teaching, but in verses 10 and 11 the emphasis is on receiving so as to be able to give more. What can you share with others in response to God's generosity to you?

> Each of you should give what you have decided in your heart to give, not reluctantly or under compulsion, for God loves a cheerful giver.
>
> **2 Corinthians 9:7**

RESPOND

'O teach me, Lord, to walk this road, / The road of simple living; / To be content with what I own / And generous in giving … / … I'd rather lose all the things of earth / To gain the things of heaven.'**

*Brian Stanley, *The History of the Baptist Missionary Society, 1792–1992*, T&T Clark, 1992
**From 'Simple Living', Stuart Townend, Keith and Kristyn Getty, Thankyou Music, 2011

Bible in a year: 1 Chronicles 28,29; Psalms 70,71

Self-defence

PREPARE

Reflect on the words: 'O, what a mystery, meekness and majesty, bow down and worship for this is your God' (Graham Kendrick, 1986, Thankyou Music).

. . . .

READ

2 Corinthians 10:1–6

EXPLORE

The Covid-19 pandemic meant that many meetings were held via Zoom; one meeting of an obscure parish council (a local government body) became an internet hit, even making the national TV news! Viewers were amazed at the unkind way in which some people, full of their own importance, spoke to each other. I wonder what people would think if some church meetings were televised!

In this final section of the letter, Paul addresses his self-important critics in Corinth but does so following Christ's example of humility and gentleness (v 1). Are there situations which you need to approach with gentleness and humility?

The church was being influenced by false teachers who said that, while he sent advice from afar, in person Paul did not appear to be a spiritual giant (vs 2,3). They were, perhaps, accusing him of being 'too worldly minded to be of any heavenly use'. Paul, however, insists that although he is down to earth, he fights with heavenly weapons (see Ephesians 6:10–20).

Christians are called to be 'in the world, but not of the world' (John 17:13–16). How do we live for Jesus without retreating from the world?

We take captive every thought to make it obedient to Christ.

2 Corinthians 10:5b

RESPOND

Individuals are often won for Christ, not with clever arguments but by seeing lives transformed, through acts of kindness and prayer. Are you trying to *persuade* someone of the truth of the gospel? Pray that God would open their eyes.

. . . .

Bible in a year: 2 Chronicles 1,2; Galatians 4

Sunday 19 June
Psalm 50

Warning to the religious

PREPARE

Pause to remember that you are coming before 'The Mighty One, God, the Lᴏʀᴅ' (Psalm 50:1).

READ

Psalm 50

EXPLORE

Throughout the Bible we see a tendency for a relationship with God to degenerate into empty religious actions and legalistic language. The prophets railed against it, Jesus spoke against it (eg Matthew 6:16) and Paul opposed it. This psalm calls God's people into a living relationship.

The picture here is of a courtroom where the holy God summons the whole of creation to observe as charges are levelled against the people of God. The Hebrew word translated 'consecrated people' in verse 5 means 'the recipients of my faithful love'* or 'those who have found grace in my sight'.** The covenant relationship God's people have with him is based on his initiative (see Deuteronomy 7:6), not earned by our actions.

Sacrifices could easily become a means of trying to earn God's favour, but we cannot provide for God's needs (vs 7–13). He wants a loving relationship where sacrifices are a demonstration of thanks to God; where his people call to him and he saves them. How do Christians try to win God's favour by religious observance?

The second charge God levels against his people is that they know and recite his laws, but do not take the action they demand (vs 16–21). The apostle James says God's Word is like a mirror, showing the things that need attention (James 1:22–25).

> 'Those who sacrifice thank-offerings honour me, and to the blameless I will show my salvation.'
>
> **Psalm 50:23**

RESPOND

If God has shown you any faults in the 'mirror' of Psalm 50, pray for his help in correcting them.

*JA Motyer, *Psalms by the Day*, Christian Focus, 2016, p131
**Amplified Bible*, Classic Edition, Zondervan, 1965

Bible in a year: 2 Chronicles 3–5; Galatians 5

Boast in the Lord

PREPARE.

'Glorify the LORD with me: let us exalt his name together' (Psalm 34:3).

- -

READ

2 Corinthians 10:7–18

EXPLORE

When Samuel was sent to anoint the future king of Israel, he thought Eliab looked the part, but God said, 'The LORD does not look at the things people look at' (1 Samuel 16:7). Some Corinthians made a similar mistake in assessing Paul's outward appearance (v 10). Paul continues his defence against the criticisms of the 'super-apostles' (see 2 Corinthians 11:5) who had become influential in Corinth. They were experts in self-promotion (v 12) but did not look beyond their own circle. They gave the impression of being authoritative but only looked to each other. They dismissed Paul because he was not outwardly impressive.

There have always been false teachers, full of self-importance. What characteristics would enable you to identify an authentic God-ordained teacher? While some wanted to belittle him, Paul's aim is to build up others (v 8).

If Paul is going to boast about any part of his ministry, it is about the Corinthians (v 13). If they criticise Paul's work, what does it say about the church in Corinth, a product of his labours?

In the parable of the talents (Matthew 25:14–30) the two servants who have wisely used treasure entrusted to them receive the commendation, 'Well done, good and faithful servant.' The only commendation which matters to Paul is that from the Lord, not self-commendation (v 18).

'Let the one who boasts boast in the Lord.'

2 Corinthians 10:17

RESPOND

Look out today for opportunities to 'boast in the Lord'. What would you tell others about him?

- -

Bible in a year: 2 Chronicles 6,7; Galatians 6

Beware of imposters

PREPARE
Ask the Lord to teach you his truths.

READ
2 Corinthians 11:1–15

EXPLORE

Does it seem an extreme reaction of Paul's to call the false apostles servants of Satan (v 15)? He is distressed about the danger that they pose to the church at Corinth. Are we too ready to accept false teaching as mere differences of opinion?

Paul is not defending himself because his feelings are hurt. He is afraid that the Corinthians are being led astray from the true faith. He has previously spoken of them as his children in the faith (eg 2 Corinthians 6:13); now he pictures himself presenting them in marriage as the bride of Christ (v 2; see also Ephesians 5:27). For the church to follow false teachings would make them unfaithful to the Lord. Just as Eve was deceived by the serpent, the Corinthians risk being led astray by false teaching. Notice how right thinking and devotion to Christ go together (v 3). How can we assess the truthfulness of teaching?

The false teachers were skilled in the rhetorical techniques of their age. In our media-driven age, does style sometimes triumph over substance in preaching? They also argued that Paul could not have been a good teacher because, unlike them, he did not ask for payment when he spoke (v 7). Although Paul argues elsewhere that church workers have a right to payment (1 Timothy 5:18), he had not accepted anything from the Corinthians, to avoid being a burden (v 9).

> I am afraid that ... your minds may somehow be led astray from your sincere and pure devotion to Christ.
>
> **2 Corinthians 11:3**

RESPOND

'Lord, "Give your servant a discerning heart ... to distinguish between right and wrong" (1 Kings 3:9). Amen.'

Suffering for Christ

PREPARE
Give thanks for Jesus' suffering for you.

· ·

READ
2 Corinthians 11:16–33

EXPLORE

Paul reluctantly answers the boasts of the 'super-apostles' with boasts of his own. He does not compete on their terms, although he is more than adequately qualified to do so. If they boasted of their Jewish racial and religious heritage, so could Paul, but he would rather boast of his sufferings. They may think that he is foolish (v 16), but Paul has told them earlier that 'the foolishness of God is wiser than human wisdom' (1 Corinthians 1:25).

We read in Acts of some of the deprivations and sufferings Paul endured for the sake of the gospel, but here he gives more details. Thirty-nine lashes and stoning were Jewish punishments, beating with rods a Roman one (vs 24,25). It seems as if everyone and everything conspires against him, but he sees suffering as a mark of his apostleship.

Most church leaders and pastors can identify with the pressures Paul felt when church members suffered. Paul's concern for the Corinthians only adds to that (v 28).

Having to escape his pursuers in a laundry basket (Acts 9:25) could have been humiliating, but a sign of weakness becomes a boast to Paul (vs 30,31). Jesus said: 'Blessed are you when people hate you ... exclude you and insult you ... because of the Son of Man ... Woe to you when everyone speaks well of you, for that is how their ancestors treated the false prophets' (Luke 6:22,26).

> If I must boast, I will boast of the things that show my weakness.
>
> **2 Corinthians 11:30**

RESPOND
Pray for the many Christians throughout the world who are suffering for their faith.

· ·

Bible in a year: 2 Chronicles 10–12; Ephesians 1

A man in Christ

PREPARE
Ask for God to reveal himself to you today.

- -

READ
2 Corinthians 12:1–10

EXPLORE

Continuing his reluctant boasting, Paul turns to his spiritual experience. Perhaps the 'super-apostles' thought that their own visions made them superior. Paul modestly talks about 'a man in Christ', but it becomes evident that he is referring to his own spectacular revelation. Jewish rabbis had various schemes of multiple heavens, but Paul seems to mean he was caught up to the presence of God (vs 2–4).

While most of us worry lest others think too little of us, Paul is afraid others may think too highly of him (vs 5,6). We know from the book of Acts that Paul received several visions, but this is the only mention of this in his letters, because he wants to be judged on words and actions. To make sure that he did not boast, Paul was given a 'thorn in the flesh' (v 7). Whatever form this weakness took, it was both a messenger from Satan and something used by God: a reminder that God can use all things for good (see Romans 8:28).

The weakness is transformed into a source of boasting, not because it is removed, but because it remains and ensures that Paul is all the more dependent upon God's grace. Rather than boast about his supernatural visions, he boasts about his frailty because it puts the focus on God's strength.

'My grace is sufficient for you, for my power is made perfect in weakness.'

2 Corinthians 12:9

RESPOND
Think of a Christian whose reliance on God's grace, despite suffering or weakness, has impressed you. Ask the Lord for strength to cope with your problems.

- -

Bible in a year: 2 Chronicles 13–15; Ephesians 2

Spiritual children

PREPARE

'May my cry come before you, Lord; give me understanding according to your word' (Psalm 119:169).

READ

2 Corinthians 12:11–21

EXPLORE

It seems that some in the church were accusing Paul of favouring other churches over them. With a little sarcasm, he points out that the only thing they have been denied is an expectation that they should contribute to his expenses (v 13). The Corinthians were his spiritual children, and as such he did not expect them to contribute to their own upbringing (v 14).

What will Paul find when he makes his next trip to Corinth? He fears that the sins about which he had to write earlier are still rife. The lifestyle of some Christians was not very different from that of the surrounding culture, and the rest of the church were too accepting of wrong behaviour. What would Paul find in the average church today?

We may be shocked at the sexual sins Paul condemns, but he is equally concerned about less spectacular problems which are found in many churches. How many Christian communities are free from 'discord, jealousy, fits of rage, selfish ambition, slander, gossip, arrogance and disorder' (v 20)? Do we take such things as seriously as we should? I once read in an old church minute book that a church member had been barred from Communion for gossiping; I wonder what the reaction would be if we tried that today!

> We have been speaking in the sight of God as those in Christ; and everything we do, dear friends, is for your strengthening.
> **2 Corinthians 12:19b**

RESPOND

Read again the list of sins in verses 20 and 21. If God challenges you, ask for his forgiveness and help.

Bible in a year: 2 Chronicles 16,17; Psalm 73

Saturday 25 June

2 Corinthians 13:1–14

Paul's prayer

PREPARE

Thank God for those Christians who have encouraged you and built up your faith.

READ

2 Corinthians 13:1–14

EXPLORE

In several places in his letters Paul gives us a revealing glimpse into his prayers for the churches he planted and served. They challenge us about our priorities in prayer.

Paul is planning to visit Corinth for a third time, and warns that, if he finds that there has been no improvement in behaviour of members of the church, they will indeed find that he can be just as tough in person as he is in his letters, contrary to the accusations of his detractors. He hopes, however, that this will not be necessary; his prayer is that Corinthians will cease from doing wrong (v 7). Matthew Henry comments: 'The most desirable thing we can ask of God, for ourselves and our friends, is to be kept from sin, that we and they may not do evil. We have far more need to pray that we may not do evil, than that we may not suffer evil.'*

Paul may be accused of weakness if the Corinthians' change of behaviour makes strong action unnecessary, but all that matters to him is that they are strong in their faith. So he prays for their restoration. While the false apostles enjoyed inflating their own status, Paul's only desire is to build up others (v 10).

Paul encourages this church to work for healing divisions and mutual encouragement before closing with the short prayer that we often use today (v 14).

We are glad whenever we are weak but you are strong; and our prayer is that you may be fully restored.

2 Corinthians 13:9

RESPOND

Who needs your prayer and encouragement today?

*Matthew Henry's Concise Commentary on the Whole Bible, Thomas Nelson, 1997

Bible in a year: 2 Chronicles 18–20; Ephesians 3

A clean slate

PREPARE

Slowly say the ancient 'Jesus Prayer': Lord Jesus Christ, Son of God, have mercy on me, a sinner.

READ

Psalm 51

EXPLORE

We once called out a carpet cleaning company to remove a stain on a rug. When done, it looked fine, but a couple of days later the stain reappeared. My wife, being a chemist, identified a key ingredient of the shampoo as a temporary bleach! The stain of sin in our lives requires permanent cleansing, not temporary hiding.

After being confronted by the prophet Nathan (2 Samuel 12:1–14), David recognised his sin and prayed this psalm. He makes no excuses but, relying on God's unfailing love and mercy, he asks God not to simply overlook his transgressions but to 'blot them out' (v 1). Sin needs to be removed and the sinner cleansed (v 2).

In saying his sin is only against God (v 4), David does not deny the dreadful things done to Bathsheba and Uriah (2 Samuel 11) but acknowledges that all sin stems from rebellion against God.

Hyssop (v 7), a plant with hairy leaves and stem, made a natural brush used for sprinkling the blood of sacrifices in Old Testament cleansing ceremonies. These pointed towards Christ's sacrifice for sin (see Hebrews 9:19–28).

Forgiveness is not just a legal state. A broken relationship is restored with the indwelling Spirit empowering us to live for God. The appropriate responses to God's forgiveness are praise and a transformed life (vs 15–17).

Have mercy on me, O God, according to your unfailing love.

Psalm 51:1a

RESPOND

Imagine the sins which trouble you being listed on a whiteboard then being wiped away. Praise God.

Bible in a year: 2 Chronicles 21–23; Ephesians 4

Kingly reading

About the writer
James Davies

James works for the Open University. He is married to Karen and they are part of a Newfrontiers church in Milton Keynes. They have three sons called Samuel, Benjamin and Joel, not much peace and quiet, and drink a lot of coffee.

The chapters we're going to read from 2 Samuel capture the tectonic plates of Israel and Judah shifting, seen in the power struggle between the 'house of Saul' and the 'house of David'. In just nine chapters, we encounter battles, grief and mourning, dishonour and unforgiveness, flawed human kings, judgement and retribution, the holiness of God and unexpected kindness lavished on a nobody.

We're going to see some wonderful qualities in King David, but we also know he's a deeply flawed, sinful man. Even in his best moments, David is only the faintest whisper of the greater King to come, Jesus, who lavishes kindness and unmerited grace not on one individual but on all who call on his name; who doesn't plan to build a temple but *is* the new temple through which we can meet with God; who doesn't seek to unify a nation but instead has won a people for God from every nation on the earth.

How can we make the most of these chapters? First, let me suggest reading the verses carefully, really believing that God has meant each one to be there, even when they perplex us! Secondly, slow down (I hope I'm not writing that only for my own sake). My life all too often proceeds at breakneck speed, but if we quiet our busy hearts, we'll hear God speak through his Word. And thirdly, read prayerfully – talk to God about what you think and what you feel, and let his Word be a springboard into his presence.

Fear of what?

PREPARE

'At the start of this series, Lord, I ask you to open my eyes to see wonderful things in your Word. Amen.'

READ

2 Samuel 1:1–16

EXPLORE

No one could claim the Bible is air-brushed or edited to give its readers a simplistic message or make everyone look good. What are we to make of today's difficult passage of grief and vengeance? Perhaps there's something here for all of us to benefit from in those times when events, life and even God don't turn out the way we expect or think they should.

We know from 1 Samuel 31 that Saul wasn't killed by the Amalekite in today's passage, no matter how elaborate the yarn he spun for David (vs 6–10). Saul had taken his own life. So why would the Amalekite lie? Very likely, to curry favour with the new king. But David's heart wasn't like others (see 1 Samuel 13:14). So instead of a self-interested glow of achievement, of having finally arrived, that might have gripped other kings' hearts (and perhaps ours, too), David was first gripped by sorrow (v 11). This wasn't a formal showing at a state occasion; David genuinely grieved for Saul and his son Jonathan (v 12). Have you ever considered the practice of fasting to express sorrow, grief or repentance? David is then moved by the fear of God and can't quite believe the Amalekite so glibly broke God's law (v 14; Psalm 105:15). The resultant execution of judgement was swift and terrible (vs 15,16).

David asked him, 'Why weren't you afraid to lift your hand to destroy the LORD's anointed?'

2 Samuel 1:14

RESPOND

'Lord, help me to both love you more and fear you more. Amen.'

Bible in a year: 2 Chronicles 24,25; Ephesians 5

Grief and honour

PREPARE
'In you, LORD my God, I put my trust' (Psalm 25:1). Do just that before you read further.

READ
2 Samuel 1:17–27

EXPLORE

For David, it's personal. Despite Saul's sin against David in the past, hounding and even trying to kill him, David honoured King Saul, the Lord's anointed. When others might have called their dead enemy weak or insecure, through unforgiveness and bitterness, instead David sang that Saul was 'mighty' and 'Israel's glory' (v 19, ESV). When some of us would have perhaps only grudgingly acknowledged Saul, David wanted the news of his death not to be known and celebrated by gloating enemies (v 20). What is David doing? He is honouring Saul, the man the Lord chose before him. What steps could you take to better honour the people around you? Is this an idea that's ever occurred to you? How might you put it into practice?

David's lament becomes even more personal about Jonathan, a man he loved as a brother, who supported and strengthened him like no one else had done in his entire life (v 26). We get the sense that David's holding nothing back in this song characterised by a devastating experience of loss. Have you ever 'put on a brave face' or tried to deny the pain of loss? That's not the example we see in David the king, or in Jesus the King of kings.

'Your glory, O Israel, is slain on your high places! How the mighty have fallen!'

2 Samuel 1:19 ESV

RESPOND
Are you in need of some help to grieve a loss? Why not reach out to someone you trust to talk and pray about this with you?

Bible in a year: 2 Chronicles 26–28; Psalm 74

Clash of kings

PREPARE
Worship Jesus before you read further, 'who, being in very nature God ... made himself nothing by taking the very nature of a servant' (Philippians 2:6,7).

READ
2 Samuel 2:1–17

EXPLORE
I marvel at David's wisdom here. How many of us have ever made a bad decision immediately after a big high or having suffered a big loss? Instead, David's instinct is to seek the Lord rather than to rashly make any significant decision (v 1). Again, we see David's integrity through his reaction to the news that the faithful men of Jabesh Gilead had buried Saul (v 4). He genuinely had not sought the kingship for personal gain or fulfilment as shown by his blessing and commitment to do good to them (vs 5,6). Is there anything in your life that you are currently pursuing too keenly and perhaps putting ahead of God?

During some situations, do you ever get the feeling, 'This is not going to end well...'? 2 Samuel 2 is exhibit A: opposing sides, young men, swords, competition... 'The battle that day was very fierce' (v 17) is probably a masterful understatement. This tragic story is repeated around the world: those in power vie for position and control – and people suffer and even die. It's likely that Saul's son, Ish-Bosheth, was a puppet for Abner who installed him as king (vs 8,9). How different to the way that Jesus taught us to serve rather than 'lord it over' others (see Matthew 20:25,26).

> 'May the Lord now show you kindness and faithfulness, and I too will show you the same favour because you have done this.'
> **2 Samuel 2:6**

RESPOND
'Be devoted to one another in love. Honour one another above yourselves' (Romans 12:10). Who can you 'honour' today?

Bible in a year: 2 Chronicles 29,30; Ephesians 6

Broken leaders

PREPARE
'Speak, Lord, for your servant is listening.'

READ
2 Samuel 2:18 – 3:5

EXPLORE

Leaders matter. And what leaders say and do matters. Joab versus Abner. David versus Ish-Bosheth. Asahel versus Abner… with terrible consequences for Asahel (2:19–23), his wasted life leaving a lasting impression on those who found him (2:23). Conflict and dispute aren't of course only between leaders – their followers, too, are often drawn into taking sides, whether in 900 BC or AD 2022. People often look at leaders for clues on what they stand for and who they should stand against.

Psalm 133 poetically describes what happens when unity among brothers is present with the promise of God's blessing. In today's passage, we see what the opposite brings: 'The war between the house of Saul and the house of David lasted a long time' (3:1) and yielded needless death, wasted lives and generation-long resentment. Over time, David's 'house' grew stronger than Saul's, but at what cost? Today, it's unlikely that you find yourself at war with anyone, but disagreement and broken relationships are perhaps likely. If you're leading formally (through the responsibility you've been given) or informally (through the influence you have on those around you), you can make a difference for good.

> The war between the house of Saul and the house of David lasted a long time. David grew stronger … while the house of Saul grew weaker…
>
> **2 Samuel 3:1**

RESPOND
'Darkness cannot drive out darkness; only light can do that. Hate cannot drive out hate; only love can do that'.*

*Martin Luther King Jr, *Strength to Love*, Harper and Row, 1963

Bible in a year: 2 Chronicles 31,32; Luke 1:1–38